Indochina Monographs

RVNAF and US Operational Cooperation and Coordination

Lt. Gen. Ngo Quang Truong

U.S. ARMY CENTER OF MILITARY HISTORY
WASHINGTON, D.C.

Library of Congress Cataloging in Publication Data

Truong, Ngo Quang.
   R.V.N.A.F. and U.S. operational cooperation and coordination.

   (Indochina monographs)
   1. Vietnamese Conflict, 1961-1975. 2. Vietnam. Quân Lu'c--History--Vietnamese Conflict, 1961-1975. 3. United States--Armed Forces--History--Vietnamese Conflict, 1961-1975. I. Title. II. Series.
DS557.7.T78   959.704'3   79-607170

This book is not copyrighted and may be reproduced in whole or in part without consulting the publisher

Reprinted 1984

CMH PUB 92-16

Indochina Monographs

This is one of a series originally published in limited quantity in 1980 by the U.S. Army Center of Military History. The continuous demand for these monographs has prompted reprinting. They were written by officers who held responsible positions in the Cambodian, Laotian, and South Vietnamese armed forces during the war in Indochina. The General Research Corporation provided writing facilities and other necessary support under an Army contract with the Center of Military History. The monographs were not edited or altered and reflect the views of their authors--not necessarily those of the U.S. Army or the Department of Defense. The authors were not attempting to write definitive accounts but to set down how they saw the war in Southeast Asia.

These works should provide useful source materials for serious historians pending publication of the more definitive series, the U.S. Army in Vietnam.

DOUGLAS KINNARD
Brigadier General, USA (Ret)
Chief of Military History

INDOCHINA MONOGRAPHS

TITLES IN THE SERIES
(title--author/s--LC Catalog Card)

The Cambodian Incursion--Brig. Gen. Tran Dinh Tho--79-21722	CMH PUB 92-4
The Easter Offensive of 1972--Lt. Gen. Ngo Quang Truong--79-20551	CMH PUB 92-13
The General Offensives of 1968-69--Col. Hoang Ngoc Lung--80-607931	CMH PUB 92-6
Intelligence--Col. Hoang Ngoc Lung--81-10844/AACR2	CMH PUB 92-14
The Khmer Republic at War and the Final Collapse--Lt. Gen. Sak Sutsakhan--79-607776	CMH PUB 92-5
Lam Son 719--Maj. Gen. Nguyen Duy Hinh--79-607101	CMH PUB 92-2
Leadership--General Cao Van Vien--80-607941	CMH PUB 92-12
Pacification--Brig. Gen. Tran Dinh Tho--79-607913	CMH PUB 92-11
RLG Military Operations and Activities in the Laotian Panhandle--Brig. Gen. Soutchay Vongsavanh--81-10934/AACR2	CMH PUB 92-19
The RVNAF--Lt. Gen. Dong Van Khuyen--79-607963	CMH PUB 92-7
RVNAF and U.S. Operational Cooperation and Coordination--Lt. Gen. Ngo Quang Truong--79-607170	CMH PUB 92-16
RVNAF Logistics--Lt. Gen. Dong Van Khuyen--80-607117	CMH PUB 92-17
Reflections on the Vietnam War--General Cao Van Vien and Lt. Gen. Dong Van Khuyen--79-607979	CMH PUB 92-8
The Royal Lao Army and U.S. Army Advice and Support--Maj. Gen. Oudone Sananikone--79-607054	CMH PUB 92-10
The South Vietnamese Society--Maj. Gen. Nguyen Duy Hinh and Brig. Gen. Tran Dinh Tho--79-17694	CMH PUB 92-18
Strategy and Tactics--Col. Hoang Ngoc Lung--79-607102	CMH PUB 92-1
Territorial Forces--Lt. Gen. Ngo Quang Truong--80-15131	CMH PUB 92-9
The U.S. Adviser--General Cao Van Vien, Lt. Gen. Ngo Quang Truong, Lt. Gen. Dong Van Khuyen, Maj. Gen. Nguyen Duy Hinh, Brig. Gen. Tran Dinh Tho, Col. Hoang Ngoc Lung, and Lt. Col. Chu Xuan Vien--80-607108	CMH PUB 92-1
Vietnamization and the Cease-Fire--Maj. Gen. Nguyen Duy Hinh--79-607982	CMH PUB 92-3
The Final Collapse--General Cao Van Vien--81-607989	CMH PUB 90-26

Preface

Over half a million US combat troops fought in South Vietnam at the height of the war. The indigenous troops they came to assist—the Republic of Vietnam Armed Forces—numbered nearly one million overall but much less than that in first line combat effective troops. In contrast to the Korean War, there was no unified command to direct the common war effort. The nature of the war itself and the environment in which it was fought were also much different from those that made up American military experience. These and other peculiarities of the Vietnam War made the effort of cooperation and coordination between American and Vietnamese combat forces an unusually complex and challenging, though rewarding, venture.

This monograph analyzes the problem areas of operational cooperation and coordination, conceived both as a command and control device to prosecute the common war effort and as a means to improve the combat effectiveness of the RVNAF. It also attempts to evaluate the successes and failures of this combined effort. As author, I am fortunate enough to be able to draw on my personal combat experience which began as platoon leader, continued through the intermediate echelons and culminated in a Corps command. Throughout my military career, I was also privileged to be associated with several distinguished US advisers with whom I enjoyed a productive working relationship and whose devoted friendship I greatly value. This has enabled me to gain insight into the subject at hand. Where my memory is short on data and statistics, I have found the documentation available particularly helpful. All the comments that I make — particularly with regard to RVNAF capabilities and leadership — reflect my own point of view as a field commander and for which I am solely responsible.

I am indebted to General Cao Van Vien, Chairman of the Joint General Staff, RVNAF, and Lieutenant General Dong Van Khuyen, Chief of Staff of the JGS, for their valuable comments on some problem areas concerning cooperation and coordination, particularly General Khuyen's contribution of his expertise in logistics. Major General Nguyen Duy Hinh, who served under me for several years as Commander of the 3d Division, is appreciated for his appropriate and always thoughtful comments. Brigadier General Tran Dinh Tho, Assistant Chief of Staff J-3, and Colonel Hoang Ngoc Lung, Assistant Chief of Staff J-2, of the JGS, each in his own field of expertise, contributed accurate data on operational planning and intelligence activities.

Finally, I am particularly indebted to Lieutenant Colonel Chu Xuan Vien and Ms. Pham Thi Bong. Lt. Colonel Vien, the last Army Attache serving at the Vietnamese Embassy in Washington, D.C., has done a highly professional job of translating, editing, and also assisting with the development of the introduction chapter. Ms. Bong, a former Captain in the Republic of Vietnam Armed Forces and also a former member of the Vietnamese Embassy staff, spent long hours typing, editing and in the administrative preparation of my manuscript in final form.

McLean, Virginia
30 September 1976

Ngo Quang Truong
Lieutenant General, ARVN

Contents

Chapter		Page
I.	INTRODUCTION	1
	The Build-Up	4
	Large Scale Operations	8
	The Phasing Down of US Combat Activities	11
	Summary of Major Events and Comments	15
II.	THE JOINT GENERAL STAFF AND MACV	18
	Role of The Joint General Staff	20
	Operational Coordination	24
	Combined Intelligence Activities	28
	Logistical Support of The RVNAF	36
III.	ARVN CORPS AND US FIELD FORCES	42
	Deployment of RVN and US Forces	42
	Organizational Arrangements for Command and Control	47
	Mission Relationships	52
IV.	RVNAF-US JOINT COMBAT OPERATIONS	63
	Operational Cooperation and Coordination Procedures	63
	Intelligence	66
	Operational Planning	69
	Assignment of Objectives, Operational Areas and Free-Fire Zones	72
	Allocation of Resources	78
	Use of Firepower	82
	Civilian Evacuation, Casualties and Property Damage	86
	Special Planning Considerations	90
	Operation Delaware/Lam Son 216	93
	Operation Lam Son 260/Nevada Eagle	105
V.	COMBINED OPERATIONS AS A MEANS OF IMPROVING ARVN COMBAT EFFECTIVENESS	115
	Objectives and Procedures	115
	The Combined Action Program	119
	Operation Fairfax/Rang Dong	128
	The Pair-Off Concept	135
	The Dong Tien (Progress Together) Program	141
	Summary and Evaluation	148

vii

Chapter	Page
VI. SOME CONSIDERATIONS AFFECTING RVNAF PERFORMANCE	152
Expansion of the US Territorial Advisory System	152
The Mobile Assistance Concept	156
Attitude of RVNAF Troops Toward Americans	161
The Tendency to Let Americans Do It All	164
Effect of One-Year Tour and Six-Month Rotation	168
VII. SUMMARY AND CONCLUSIONS	172
GLOSSARY	184

Tables

No.		
1.	Civilian Casualties and Causes	87

Charts

1.	RVN Military Organization, 1966	21
2.	Organization, Joint Operations Center, JGS	27
3.	RVN Territorial Command and Control	44
4.	Arrangement for Combined Command and Control, ICTZ, April 1968	51
5.	Command Relationships	53
6.	Configuration of Tactical Zones and Areas	74
7.	Task Organization, Operation LAM SON 260/NEVADA EAGLE	108
8.	Coordination and Control, Combined Action Program	122
9.	Organization, Province Advisory Team	154

Maps

1.	Deployment of Major Logistical Commands	37
2.	Deployment of Major ARVN and US Units, March 1966	48
3.	1966 Combined Campaign Objectives	55
4.	Operation DELAWARE/LAM SON 216	95
5.	Operation LAM SON 260/NEVADA EAGLE	110
6.	Combined Action Program, ICTZ, November 1969	121
7.	FAIRFAX/RANG DONG Area of Operation, 1967	130
8.	Pair-Off Operations, II CTZ	138
9.	DONG TIEN Areas of Operation, III CTZ	143

Illustrations

Arrival of the 173d Airborne Brigade, Bien Hoa, 5 May 1965	14
Departure of the Last US Combat Unit, Da Nang, March 1973	14
Some Communist Trucks and Weapons Captured in the A Shau Valley, 1968	103
Pair-Off Senior Commanders Conference, II CTZ	137
Dong Tien Joint Tactical Operations Center, Tay Ninh	137
Fairfax Operation, Gia Dinh Province	145
Dong Tien Commanders Planning an Operation	146
A Mobile Advisory Team, 1968	160
Artillery Advisor and Counterpart During Drill	160

CHAPTER I

Introduction

The war in South Vietnam took a momentous step forward in March 1965 when US combat troops were committed to the land war. This occurred just five months after the first US airstrike was unleashed against North Vietnam as a result of the Maddox incident in the Gulf of Tonkin and other escalated actions by the enemy in the South. By this time the American effort to help the shaky government of South Vietnam to meet the increasing Communist military threat had been built up to approximately 23,000 men, mostly assigned to field advisory teams and combat support units. The decision that President Johnson and the US Congress made to reaffirm US commitment to the Republic of Vietnam was a bold and fateful step. For the first time in the war, US ground troops were sent to Vietnam, not only to advise and support their Vietnamese ally, but also to destroy the enemy. A new era was about to open which saw the American and Vietnamese combat troops fight hand in hand in a succession of campaigns designed not only to destroy the enemy but also to bolster the capabilities of the faltering Republic of Vietnam Armed Forces (RVNAF) as well.

This radical departure of US policy toward South Vietnam did not stem from an expansionist design. Rather it was forced on the United States by the gravity of a deteriorating situation. For one thing, the five-year old counter-insurgency war had definitely escalated to a new level and its nature had changed with the introduction of full strength regimental units from the North Vietnamese regular Army (NVA) and the activation of division-size units in the South, such as the CT-9. The Viet Cong forces, increasingly replenished with North Vietnamese troops, began to receive modern weapons from the Communist Bloc, such as the AK-47 assault rifle and the RPG-2 rocket launcher. From all indications, the enemy seemed to be entering an important phase of his strategy and was on the verge of winning the war after his resounding victory at Binh Gia. Military strategists—American and Vietnamese alike—were concerned about the possibility of a Communist wedge being driven across the country from the Pleiku-Kontum area to Qui Nhon. This action, if successful, would effectively cut South Vietnam into two parts along National Route QL-19 and create favorable conditions for the enemy to achieve further victories. The whole process, it was feared, could eventually lead to the disruption of the RVNAF and the consequent collapse of South Vietnam. In addition, the overall political and military situation of the Republic of Vietnam (RVN) was deteriorating at an alarming rate.

Only one year and a half had elapsed since President Ngo Dinh Diem was overthrown on 1 November 1963. His overthrow ushered in a period of turmoil marked by internal power struggles, factionalism, and divisiveness. The armed forces lost essential unity of purpose and solidarity which took months, if not years, to restore. The reign of the Revolutionary Military Council led by General Duong Van Minh lasted only three ephemeral months; it ended with the arrest of the Council key members in a bloodless coup staged by General Nguyen Khanh who installed himself as Prime Minister. His first act was a wholesale purge to consolidate his power. Still unable to rally support for his one-man rule, Khanh maneuvered to establish a "triumvirate" military leadership including himself, General Minh and General Tran Thien Khiem, and appointed a civilian prime minister. To give credibility to a form of "democratic" rule, an assembly of politicians and notables was created under the name of "National High Council" whose given role was half-legislative, half-consultative. But the true political power still lay in the hands of the "Armed Forces Council" composed of a select group of emerging, young, and ambitious men. It was this collective military leadership that replaced the ineffective triumvirate, appointed the Chief of State, and later dissolved the National High Council which had begun to infringe on the generals' power.[1]

The whole period in retrospect seemed to tear the country apart and turn the army into an arena of power struggle and political intrigues. The machinations and upheavals in Saigon made their rippling effect felt throughout the hierarchy. Unit commanders no longer dedicated themselves to the task of fighting the enemy; they spent their time and energy switching loyalty to save their own skins. Plagued by distrust and petty bickering, the military leadership failed to rally popular support and impart sense and direction to the war effort. In the countryside, the Strategic Hamlet system which heretofore had provided some measure of territorial security almost completely fell apart due to neglect. Its impetus was gone and many outlying areas relapsed into the grips of the enemy infrastructure. In several instances, Regional and Popular Forces (RF and PF) commanders struck a tacit "live and let live" arrangement with local Communists. The total RVNAF force structure was 500,000 by the end of 1964 but this was just a nominal figure, not indicative of real combat strength. By any standards, overall effectiveness of the RVNAF was markedly on the decline. Poorly motivated and poorly led, RVNAF units were hardly a match for their determined and better-disciplined foes.

All in all, this was a dark period of time whose events threatened the very survival of the RVN, and as a direct consequence, brought about the increasing commitment of US combat troops to the land war which was to be carried into new heights over the next few years.

---

[1] This high-handed coup prompted US Ambassador Maxwell D. Taylor to use the rather undiplomatic method of dressing down the Vietnamese generals for their unsettling action. The US was striving during this time to restore political stability in South Vietnam.

The Build-Up

Upon recommendations of General William C. Westmoreland, Commander of the US Military Assistance in Vietnam (USMACV), the United States government agreed to deploy combat forces to South Vietnam to ward off the imminent disaster faced by the RVN.

On March 8, 1965, the first major US combat unit, the 9th Marine Amphibious Brigade, arrived in Da Nang to provide protection for the airbase there which, because of increased air strikes against North Vietnam, had become a major target for enemy sabotage. It was soon followed in May by the US Army 173d Airborne Brigade, which was deployed to Bien Hoa and Vung Tau for the same purpose: security for airbases. These initial combat contingents were to prepare the groundwork for the rapid buildup which soon followed with the arrival of other major US units and the expansion of airfields, ports, and logistics bases throughout the country.

June and July 1965 were the months of most significant events. The four-month old civilian government under Chief of State Phan Khac Suu and Prime Minister Phan Huy Quat resigned as a result of irreconcilable differences between the two leaders. It was decided that the Armed Forces Council would take over. Apparently leaderless since its chairman, General Khanh, was ousted and expatriated in February as a result of his dictatorial actions, the Council voted to install Lieutenant General Nguyen Van Thieu, then Minister of Defense, as Chairman of the National Leadership Committee (Chief of State or President) and Major General Nguyen Cao Ky, Commander of the Vietnamese Air Force, as Chairman of the Central Executive Committee (Prime Minister). The inauguration of the Thieu-Ky government brought back some measure of political stability and ended the period of turmoil. General Ky's high-handed methods, however, gradually eroded the relationship between himself and General Thieu and led to their ultimate split in 1971. On the battlefield, the Vietnamese Army suffered its second major setback at Dong Xoai since Binh Gia in late December 1964 at the hand of the same enemy, the CT-9 Division. Two battalions were virtually destroyed, including the 6th Airborne Battalion. It was in June that B-52 bombers, in addition to tactical jets, were used for the first time to destroy enemy bases. The results were impressive, and B-52 strikes were to become a most successful means of air support in the years to follow.

In the meantime, the arrival of the III US Marine Amphibious Force in South Vietnam enabled the US Military Assistance Command to proceed with the development of major bases. Chu Lai was the first base and jet airfield complex to be created out of wilderness by the Marine Seabees. Construction work also began on the major logistics bases at Cam Ranh Bay, Qui Nhon and Da Nang after they had been secured by US combat forces. This was a time of accelerated buildup. During the month of July, the 2d Brigade of the 1st US Infantry Division arrived at Long Binh, soon to be transformed into one of the largest logistics base complexes in South Vietnam.[2] It was followed by the 1st Brigade of the 101st Airborne Division which was deployed to Cam Ranh Bay where the construction of a port and an airfield were transforming it into a major logistics complex of the 2d CTZ.

In September, the entire US 1st Air Cavalry Division arrived at Qui Nhon and deployed to An Khe where it established its operational base. Late in December, the 3d Brigade of the 25th Infantry Division closed in and deployed to the vicinity of Pleiku, seat of the Headquarters, II Corps, RVNAF. By year end, US military strength in Vietnam had reached above the 150,000 mark to include 92,000 Army, 8,000 Navy, 37,000 Marines and 14,000 Air Force. The pace of the buildup had been set and was carried into 1966.

On February 6, 1966, President Johnson arrived in Honolulu to confer with leaders of the RVN government. The conference strengthened the pledge by both governments to defeat Communist aggression and bring about social betterment of South Vietnam.

In March, a serious political crisis erupted in Hue and Da Nang. Militant Buddhists joined by radical students staged demonstrations

---

[2] The entire 1st Infantry Division completed its deployment by October the same year.

demanding more rapid progress toward elective government. Some ARVN units, like the 1st Infantry Division and the Rangers sided with the Buddhists and it appeared that the I Corps Commander, Lieutenant General Nguyen Chanh Thi, was also behind the move. It was feared the movement could turn into open armed rebellion and disrupt the war effort. As a result, General Thi was relieved of his command and replaced by a rapid succession of three Corps Commanders who were all removed after refusing to repress the rebels.[3] Finally Vietnamese marines and paratroopers were surreptiously brought to Da Nang by US cargo and Vietnamese commercial planes and they finally quelled the rebellion.

By late April, the US 25th Infantry Division had completed its deployment to South Vietnam and was stationed in Hau Nghia province where it established its base camp at Cu Chi. In August, the 196th Light Infantry Brigade arrived and soon operated in Tay Ninh province. It was followed by the US 4th Infantry Division which completed its deployment in October and was assigned to the Kontum-Pleiku area where it established its base camp at Mount Ham Rong. With the arrival of the 199th Light Infantry Brigade in the Saigon area and the first elements of the US 9th Infantry Division which was eventually to establish a base camp at Dong Tam in Dinh Tuong province, total US military strength in South Vietnam, by year end, had reached 385,000 men.

The period of buildup was marked by joint efforts of the United States and five other allies—the Republic of Korea, Thailand, Australia, the Philippines and New Zealand—to firm up their resolution to help South Vietnam resist Communist aggression. This was the object of the "Manila Conference" held on October 24, during which the allies pledged that their military forces would be withdrawn as the other side withdrew its forces to the north, ceased infiltration, and the level of

---

[3] These commanders were: Major General Nguyen Van Chuan, Lieutenant General Ton That Dinh, and Major General Huynh Van Cao, all natives of Central Vietnam. Finally, Major General Hoang Xuan Lam, commander of the 2d Infantry Division, was designated I Corps Commander. He remained in this job until early 1972.

violence thus subsided. President Johnson who attended this meeting took time out to make a surprise visit to US troops in Cam Ranh on October 26.

The build up of US and allied forces in South Vietnam, it has been said, was a determined effort to defeat aggression on the one hand, and to help South Vietnam to consolidate, expand and improve its armed forces on the other. Toward this goal, US forces, after a period of familiarization with the environment, began to conduct operations with the participation of ARVN forces. The majority of these combined operations were campaigns lasting from a few weeks to several months during which ARVN forces mostly played a secondary role, their commitment rarely exceeding the size of a regiment.

The first major engagement involving US and ARVN troops of II Corps occurred in October 1965 in the Central Highlands, where the enemy had assembled three regiments and attacked the Plei Me border camp, west of Pleiku. Then, during the month of November, the US 1st Air Cavalry Division and ARVN troops were engaged in a major battle in the Ia Drang valley from which they came out as victors.

Beginning in 1966, combined US-RVN military effort shifted toward populated centers where a major task of pacification was being emphasized by the RVN government. However, the exposure of US combat forces to the populace was deemed undesirable by the RVN government for political and psychological reasons. Barely ten years had elapsed since the last French troops had departed. Apparently, it would tarnish the image of national independence and suzerainty if foreign troops made their appearance among the population. This was a dilemma for the RVN government, torn between its concern for outward propriety and the indispensable commitment of foreign troops, which finally prevailed. The largest of such commitments took place in Tay Ninh province where the US 1st and 4th Infantry Divisions, the 173d ABN Brigade and several ARVN battalions defeated the NVA CT-9 and drove it back into Cambodia. In Binh Dinh province, ARVN forces in cooperation with the US 1st Air Cavalry Division and Korean units succeeded in decimating the NVA "Gold Star" Division (later designated 3d Division) and driving it away from the northern half of the province. In the first CTZ, US and RVN Marines conducted a successful combined operation against the NVA 324B Division in Quang Tri province.

By year end, total enemy combat strength in South Vietnam had increased to over 282,000. This included about 58,000 men infiltrated from North Vietnam during the year, an indication of increasing reliance on NVA replacements. The enemy now committed entire regiments in battle and sometimes a full or even reinforced division. This was to presage a new period of major engagements pitting the now modernized VC-NVA units against ARVN and US troops whose total strength approximated the one million mark.

Large Scale Operations

One of the major tasks undertaken by the US Military Assistance Command in South Vietnam during this period of major engagements was the qualitative and quantitative improvement of the RVN Armed Forces. At the end of 1966, total RVNAF strength stood at 633,645 men including nearly 300,000 Regional and Popular Forces. This strength was to increase by 122,000 during the first half of 1968 as a result of general mobilization. It was also during this period that improvement and modernization programs were initiated and their implementation accelerated in the wake of the Tet offensive. It was not until mid-1968 that for the first time the RVNAF were entirely equipped with M-16 rifles. There is no doubt that the RVNAF came of age during this period and emerged from it as a full-fledged military force, capable of sharing the combat burden with US forces on an equal basis and ready to take on new responsibilities.

The improved performance on the part of the RVNAF was due in part to combined operational campaigns during which combat skills and teamwork were learned and developed in keeping with standards set by US forces. Whereas the joint US-RVN Combined Campaign Plan—developed each year since late 1965—provided the division of tasks and coordination of the overall effort, it was the concept behind the actual execution of this plan that made it work. Whether called "Buddy System" or

"Combined Action," it afforded the opportunity for ARVN forces to observe and evaluate the combat standards displayed by US units in action. This was one of the primary objectives of combined operations of all sizes. Still, throughout this period, the RVNAF were only primarily responsible for area security in support of pacification while US forces sought out and destroyed main enemy units.

In the III Corps area, Operation FAIRFAX, conceived under this tutelage concept, paired off and integrated three US battalions with those of the ARVN 5th Ranger Group down to the squad level. The campaign lasted the entire year of 1967. While it was deemed a success, in essence it was an operation planned and directed by US forces and while the integration of forces down to the lowest level proved to be beneficial, it certainly did not help enhance ARVN capabilities for planning and conducting combat operations on their own. Thus it was decided to concentrate on combined operations in which US and ARVN units operated side-by-side in close coordination and in direct support of each other. ARVN units would thus benefit from additional helicopter, artillery, air and logistical support which was amply provided by US units.

In January 1967, Operation CEDAR FALLS was launched into the "Iron Triangle" and Long Nguyen enemy base areas, during which US troops of the 1st Infantry Division, the 173d ABN Brigade and 11th Cavalry Regiment and several ARVN battalions discovered and destroyed a vast underground shelter complex of the enemy's T-4 Military Region. In February, another major combined operation, code-named "JUNCTION CITY," was directed against War Zone C in Tay Ninh province. In this operation, US forces of the 1st and 25th Infantry Division, the 173d Brigade, the 11th Armored Cavalry Regiment and the 196th Light Infantry Brigade flushed out and destroyed major enemy combat units while the ARVN 5th, 25th, 18th Divisions and elements of the ABN Division and the Marine Brigade maintained a security cordon near the populated areas. The operation continued until mid-May and ended with resounding successes.

In 1968, in keeping with the same concept of mutual support and coordination, operation TRUONG CONG DINH was conducted in March in Dinh Tuong and Kien Tuong provinces with the participation of the US

9th Infantry Division. It was followed by Operation QUYET THANG, conducted in the Saigon area and involving elements of the US 1st, 9th and 25th Divisions and the ARVN 5th and 25th Division, and Airborne and Marine troops. Then in April, the US 101st ABN Division and the 3d Brigade, 82d ABN Division, in conjunction with the ARVN 1st Infantry Division, operated in the lowland of Quang Tri and Thua Thien provinces in operation CARENTAN II. Operation TOAN THANG, which was followed by TOANG THANG II in the Capital Military District, was conducted next with a combination of ARVN III Corps and US II Field Force units. Also, in April, the ARVN 1st Infantry Division in coordination with the US 1st Air Cavalry Division launched Operation DELAWARE/LAM SON 216 into the A Shau Valley to pre-empt enemy preparations for an attack on Hue.

By far the greatest challenge during this period of time was the enemy's country-wide Tet offensive campaign launched on January 31, 1968, against 36 provincial capitals, 5 major cities, including Saigon and Hue, and 64 district towns. It was followed in May by another wave of attacks, but in both phases of the offensive, the enemy was dealt a resounding military defeat. The longest battle was fought around the citadel of Hue and the final success of ARVN units in reoccupying the city was again an outstanding example of combined effort and mutual support between US Marine units and ARVN troops.

It was also during this period of large scale engagements that the US followed up with the deployment of additional units and nearly completed the buildup of US forces in South Vietnam by the end of 1968. The US 9th Division, part of which had arrived in December 1966, completed its deployment in January 1967. It was followed in September by activation of the 23d Infantry Division (Americal) based at Chu Lai. Then in November 1967 the entire 101st ABN Division arrived. Its 1st Brigade had been operating in South Vietnam since the early buildup more than two years earlier. The last major combat units brought into South Vietnam were the 3d Brigade of the 82d ABN Division which arrived in February 1968 and the 1st Brigade of the 5th Infantry Division, which arrived in July the same year. Thus by the end of 1968, total US military strength in South Vietnam had passed the half million mark (536,040) with 113 maneuver battalions. During the same period, RVNAF forces were built up to a ceiling of 826,500 men (including about 393,000 RF and PF troops), and a total of 160 maneuver battalions.

The RVN, meanwhile, succeeded in consolidating its political base by inaugurating the 2d Republic with President Nguyen Van Thieu and Vice President Nguyen Cao Ky, who were elected on 3 September 1967, along with members of the Senate of the National Assembly. The installation of the Lower House followed in October and completed the process of democratizing the military rule that had begun in November 1963. On the US side, General William C. Westmoreland was appointed US Army Chief of Staff and left Vietnam for his new post on 30 June 1968 after serving four distinguished years as Commander, US Military Assistance Command, Vietnam. He was succeeded by General Creighton W. Abrams, who assumed command on 3 July 1968.

The Phasing Down of US Combat Activities

The political impact of the enemy Tet offensive in 1968 brought about far-reaching developments in US policy concerning the war in Vietnam. While President Johnson emphasized in Honolulu in July 1968 that the US would pursue the war at the current pace if North Vietnam did not curtail its aggression, there were indications that he was inclined toward bringing about peace through negotiations. The stop-and-go bombing orders frequently issued by the US President constituted an effort toward this end but did not succeed in bringing the Communists to the negotiation table until he decided to step down. As soon as President Nixon took office, he entered into secret negotiations with North Vietnam toward what he had promised: ending the war and bringing home US troops. At the same time, in keeping with his doctrine of self-determination and emphasis on the role the allies were to play in common defense, which he formulated in the Midway conference on 8 June 1969, he also ordered the initial redeployment of 25,000 US troops as the

first step of the withdrawal process. This action, in concert with
other US efforts to accelerate the turn-over of equipment and the RVNAF
Improvement and Modernization Plan, including the building up of RVNAF
force level, was part of a preconceived program, conveniently called
"Vietnamization" and aimed at disengaging US combat troops from Vietnam
and turning over combat responsibilities to the RVNAF. Thus, from a
peak of 549,500 on April 30, total US troop strength in South Vietnam
began to decrease in preplanned increments until, by the end of 1969,
it had been reduced by 110,000 men. Over the next year, 1970, each
successive announcement to the effect that the RVNAF had markedly improved
was accompanied by a parallel reduction in US force so that by year end
total US strength stood at only 335,000. Then, over the next two years,
the unilateral withdrawal of US troops was kept up at a continuous
pace, diminishing US strength by half at the end of 1971 until it was
reduced to a token figure of 24,000 a month before the Paris Agreement
was signed.

The redeployment of US forces from Vietnam during this period of
time was also paralleled by substantial reductions in B-52 sorties,
tactical air, and naval support, and the gradual transfer of US bases
and other facilities to the RVNAF. Thus, in a sense, US combat operations were progressively reduced beginning in 1969 and as far as US
forces were concerned, appeared to be just delaying actions pending redeployment. It seemed that, according to public announcements, MACV was
satisfied with the improvements made by the RVNAF during the previous
years and believed that they could carry on with only modest support
from US forces.

But still, in keeping with the tutelage concept and under the pressure
of Vietnamization, combined operations continued throughout the period,
although spaced further apart, and with less and less US troop commitment. It appeared that US forces were gradually reverting to their pre-involvement role of combat support. Operation SPEEDY EXPRESS, which
ended in May 1969 after 6 months of activities was perhaps the last
major engagement of US troops in the Mekong Delta. In III Corps tactical
zone operation TOAN THANG, Phase 3, which lasted from February to October
1969 was crowned with success, but the US 1st Infantry Division which

participated in it began to stand down pending redeployment in April 1970. By the end of 1970, the US 4th and 25th Infantry Divisions were redeployed, thus leaving the III Corps area and the Central Highlands virtually void of major US combat units. And when 1971 ended, there was no longer any division-size US combat unit in the country, except for the 101st ABN Division (-) in Phu Bai.

The last major joint US-RVN combat venture was the cross-border operation into Cambodia on 30 April 1970 aimed at destroying COSVN headquarters and enemy sanctuaries. It was followed by two other operations in May, involving a total of 50,000 US and ARVN troops, and ended on 30 June. In September, the US Marines Combined Action force was inactivated, ending US Marine combined combat activites in I Corps area. In January 1971, the US Special Forces turned over to the RVNAF the last of its border camps in the Central Highlands after more than 5 years of operations. On 8 February 1971, the ARVN I Corps, augmented by the Airborne and the Marine Divisions launched operation LAM SON 719 into Laos with the objective of disrupting NVA logistical installations along the Ho Chi Minh trail. Although it was a combined effort of major proportions involving substantial air and helicopter support, no US combat troops went into Laos; they were only deployed to provide security and set up lines of communication to support the RVNAF on the friendly side of the border.

Combat activities during this period of US force standdown culminated in the enemy summer offensive of 1972 during which Quang Tri provincial city and the district towns of Loc Ninh in MR-3 and Dakto, Tam Quan, and Bong Son, in MR-2 were lost. With effective support of B-52 sorties, however, the RVNAF succeeded in relieving An Loc after a month-long siege and warded off the enemy threat against Kontum. Also with extensive US naval and air firepower support, the Vietnamese Marines finally reoccupied Quang Tri city on 15 September 1972.[4]

---

[4] The Marines actually penetrated Quang Tri citadel and physically reoccupied it in the afternoon of 15 September, but the RVN flag was officially hoisted over the citadel only at 1000 hours the following day.

Arrival of the 173d Airborne Brigade, Bien Hoa, 5 May 1965

Departure of the last US combat unit (3-21 Battalion, 196th Light Infantry Brigade), Da Nang, March 1973.

On 28 June 1972, Géneral Fred C. Weyand assumed the duties of Commander, US Military Assistance, Vietnam, replacing General Creighton W. Abrams who returned to the United States to be US Army Chief of Staff. The phasing down of US involvement through the Vietnamization process was completed in November 1972 with a crash program of equipment stock-up for the RVNAF in anticipation of a cease-fire.

Summary of Major Events and Comments

The US active involvement in the Vietnam war was a relatively short but highly effective venture. By the time it ended, the major objectives it set about to accomplish had been reached; there was no doubt about it. In the first place, US engagement in both the air and ground wars had averted the almost certain loss of South Vietnam and set back North Vietnam's plan to conquer the South for several years. Second, US direct intervention had helped stabilize the political turmoil and restore constitutional government and democracy to South Vietnam thus creating favorable conditions for self-determination, a principle the United States always advocated. Finally, the effectiveness of US air power, the combat performance of US ground troops, and the availability of US logistical facilities helped consolidate, improve, and expand the capabilities of the RVNAF to the extent that they finally emerged as a viable force capable—under certain conditions—of defending the nation.

Throughout the years of US involvement, several events of far-reaching importance came to affect the course of the war, the tactics used to fight it, and eventually the outcome of the war itself.

The buildup of US combat forces was a quick-reaction move designed to avert an imminent danger rather than to win the war. The US sent troops to South Vietnam with the reservation that they would be withdrawn as soon as the enemy showed signs of relenting on his aggression. Although US troop strength reached a peak of 549,500 in April 1969, this peak was never maintained for any length of time. Like a perfect parabolic curve, the buildup came down just as soon as it reached its apex, and the curve downward was just as unrelenting as the curve upward.

One might speculate, from hindsight, what would have been the course of the war had US strength been maintained for a few years longer. Then, the withdrawal of US troops could have been carried out more slowly, thus affording the RVNAF the chance to fill in the void, in terms of combat units, firepower, mobility and psychological conditioning.

The use of B-52 bombers to support ground troops was a marvelous tactical innovation that helped turn around the outcome of many battles. The fact that it had been used for so long and so unfailingly in every case turned it into a major psychological factor that sustained the morale of the RVNAF in the field. In time, it became a central tactical factor on which our field commanders relied, perhaps unduly, in their battle plans. The same could be said of US firepower in general, whether provided by jet fighters, artillery or naval guns. It was unfortunate that this firepower support was also reduced along with ground troops whereas it could have been selectively maintained to keep the tactical balance unimpaired.

Over the period of US involvement, the RVNAF almost doubled in size if not in capabilities. This rapid expansion and modernization was made possible by general mobilization and the several Improvement and Modernization plans implemented. While it was true that this was an impressive increase of the overall force structure, figures might be misleading. For one thing, the number of combat units did not increase in any substantial way. The 18th Infantry Division which was activated in 1966 was largely a consolidation of independent regiments and the 3d Division was only created as late as 1971. Several additional Ranger groups were organized indeed but they lacked the firepower and combat footing of divisions, which constitute the true backbone of any army. For another, the strength of the regular forces was only less than half of the RVNAF total strength. Even then the ratio of logistics and support troops to combat troops was such that the RVNAF in the end did not enjoy any significant increase in overall combat strength. Also, the rapid numerical buildup could only have been achieved at the detriment of the quality of troops and lower echelon leaders, for no amount of training could, in a relatively short time, turn out experienced leaders and combat-tested troops.

Finally, the advent of combined operations conceived and carried out under the tutelage concept, although salutary in its overall effect, hardly helped to enhance Vietnamese planning capabilities. In the planning stage, US commanders usually tended to keep it all to themselves, thus relegating their Vietnamese counterparts to the role of blindfolded executors. This was understandable enough given the possible leaks on the part of the Vietnamese, and the fact that combat assets were largely under US control. Operational plans on the Vietnamese side were sometimes merely translations of US orders. In addition, the tactical role played by RVNAF units was largely a secondary one and only became a major one when US troops redeployed. Then there were other difficulties arising from the mere fact that US troops were total strangers, racially, culturally and mentally different from the indigenous people they had come to help.

These and other facets of the problem, US operational cooperation and coordination, their successes and failures, strengths and weaknesses, are the things this monograph proposes to elucidate.

CHAPTER II

The Joint General Staff and MACV

The introduction of US combat and other allied forces in the Vietnam ground war to fight alongside the Republic of Vietnam Armed Forces gave rise to problems of coordination and control. Given the size and diversity of forces committed, military leaders at first were inclined toward some form of unified command of the multi-national United Nations or NATO type. In April 1965, General Westmoreland, commander US MACV, suggested the idea of a combined US-RVN command with an American general officer in charge, assisted by a Vietnamese deputy or chief of staff. For political reasons, however, the US MACV commander thought that this combined command should be gradually and quietly introduced.

The idea of a combined command appeared to receive wide acceptance among top Vietnamese leaders when it was first suggested. They felt that this arrangement offered an ideal arrangement for prosecuting the war which somehow was going to be the primary responsibility of US forces. The divisiveness amidst the Vietnamese military leadership and the deteriorating situation at the time also seemed to favor this arrangement. In time, however, this attitude became less enthusiastic as Vietnamese leaders grew more aware of their role and responsibility, and most particularly, of the attitudes among the population whom they were trying to rally to the national cause. Sensing this changing attitude, the US dropped the matter altogether and withdrew the recommendation concerning the US-RVN combined command.

In keeping with the US avowed policy of self-determination and his mission in particular, General Westmoreland explained the rationale behind his decision:

I consistently resisted suggestions that a simple, combined command could more effectively prosecute the war. I believed that subordinating the Vietnamese forces to US control would stifle the growth of leadership and acceptance of responsibility essential to the development of Vietnamese forces capable eventually of defending their country. Moreover, such a step would be counter to our basic objective of assisting Vietnam in a time of emergency and of leaving a strong, independent country at the time of our withdrawal. Subordination also might have given credence to the enemy's absurd claim that the United States was no more than a colonial power. I was also fully aware of the practical problems of forming and operating a headquarters with an international staff.[1]

Opting for cooperation and coordination instead of a unified command, General Westmoreland must have carefully balanced the pros and cons. The intimate cooperation between MACV and the JGS and his close relationship with his counterpart, and the fact that the US was providing the RVNAF with equipment and logistical support notwithstanding a substantial increase in MACV budget, all these could exercise as many direct influences on the RVNAF and the conduct of the war as would a combined command, and without its disadvantages. Under a combined command in addition to the political and psychological handicaps mentioned earlier, US forces might run the risk of losing some freedom of action, and the pressure exerted through such a command might well lead to an even more extensive American participation in the war. This was not what the US had set about to do in Vietnam.

And so the concept of cooperation and coordination took over. It was based on the principle of equal partnership and a harmonious division of tasks. US forces were to assume the primary burden of the war—searching out and destroying enemy main forces—while the RVN armed forces concentrated on supporting pacification and eliminating the enemy infrastructure. Paradoxical as it might seem to traditionalists, the concept of cooperation and coordination proved to be sound and effective for immediate purposes as well as for the ultimate goal of developing the RVNAF capabilities to defend their country.

---

[1] *Report on the War in Vietnam*, "Section II: Report on Operations in South Vietnam, January 1964-June 1968," by General W. S. Westmoreland, Commander, US MACV.

At the national level, this concept worked well between MACV and the Joint General Staff due to the harmonious relationship between their commanders. Anxious on its part to assume the war role on equal terms and to give new sense and direction to the command and control of the RVNAF, the RVN government designated Lieutenant General Cao Van Vien as Chairman of the Joint General Staff in October 1965, and later elevated him to four-star rank. The affable personality of General Vien, his professional competence and his apolitical attitude were qualities that made him a fine counterpart of General Westmoreland, a dedicated professional soldier and diplomat. To ensure even closer coordination, General Westmoreland designated as his personal representative to the JGS, Brigadier General James L. Collins, Jr., who was senior adviser of the RVNAF territorial forces. This close relationship was to produce excellent results in the combined effort of prosecuting the war and greatly inspired subordinate commanders and staffs of both countries.

Role of the Joint General Staff

As command body of the RVN armed forces, the Joint General Staff was the focus of cooperation and coordination between the RVN and the US forces in South Vietnam. Since the RVNAF force structure increased rapidly during the years of US participation, the JGS also underwent a substantial development in staff strength, although its basic organization remained the same. *(Chart 1)* Its general staff divisions almost paralleled those of MACV whose chiefs served as advisers. Staff coordination between the JGS and MACV was performed either on an ad-hoc basis or on a fixed schedule, determined by mutual agreement. Major areas of interest included, as far as the JGS was concerned:

JGS	MACV	
J-1	J-1	Manpower resources, mobilization and replacements, armed strength and force structure plan.
J-2	J-2	Situation estimates and intelligence plans.
J-7	J-2	Technical intelligence collection.
J-3	J-3	Annual combined campaign plans - Contingency plans - US air and naval support. Organization, expansion and modernization of units.

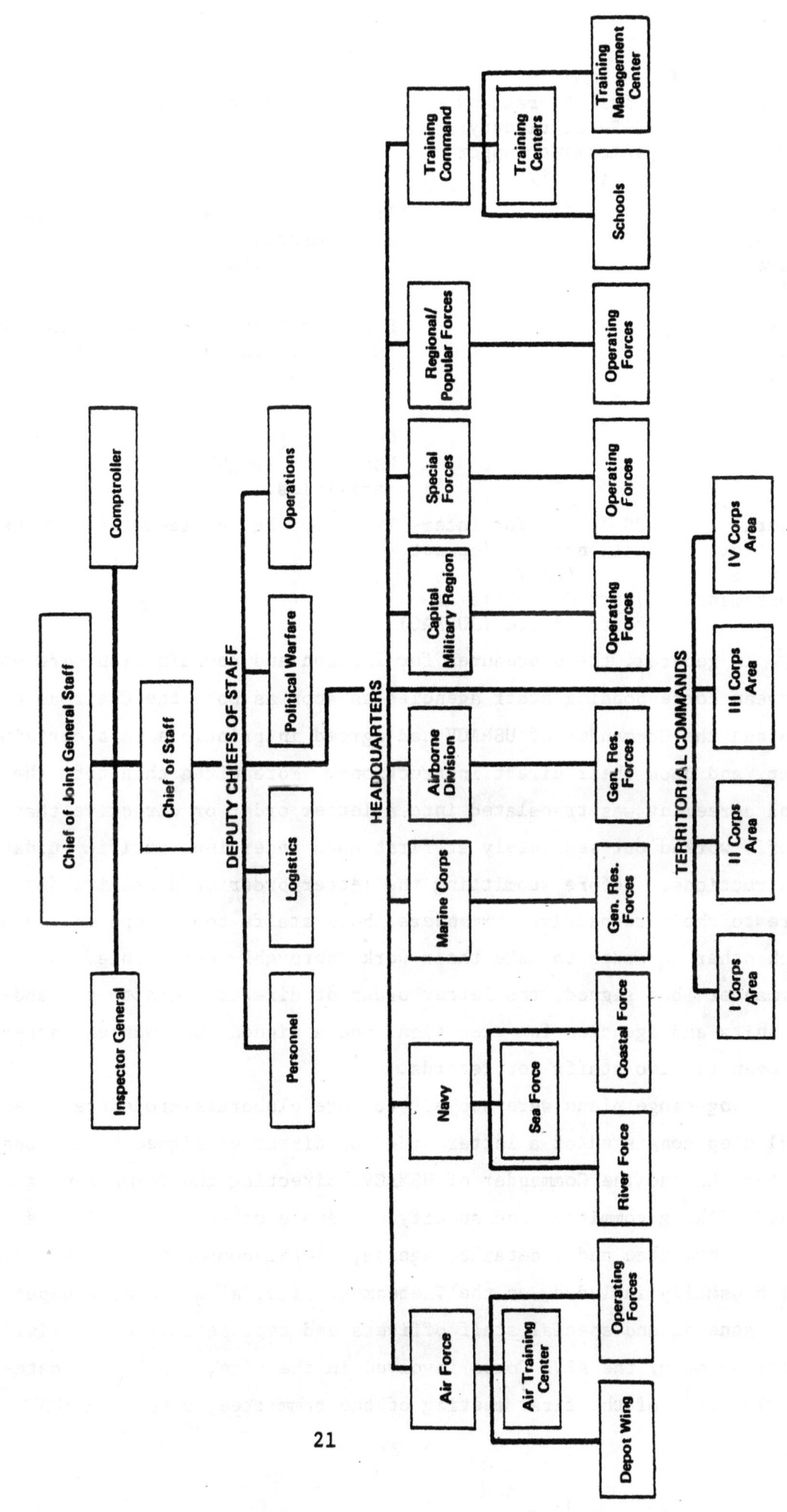

CHART 1—RVN MILITARY ORGANIZATION, 1966

J-3	Civil Operations and Revolutionary Development Support (CORDS)	Combined plans for pacification support.
Central Training Command (CTC)	J-3	Training plans and programs, in-country and overseas.
Central Logistical Command (CLC)	J-4	Logistical support plans. Use of US assets to compensate for RVNAF shortages. Equipping of units.
J-6	J-6	Communications-electronics plans. Use of US long-line communications facilities.
General Political Warfare Department	US Agency for International Development (USAID) Joint US Public Affairs Office (JUSPAO)	Troop morale, civic-action and psyops.

In general, the procedures for liaison and coordination were established between corresponding staff agencies as soon as both the Chairman of the JGS and the Commander of USMACV had agreed in principle on a certain subject, and upon their direct instructions. More often than not, the command agreement was translated into a letter order or directive that both staffs worked out separately at first upon receiving specific guidance instructions. Before submitting the letter order or directive for signature to their respective commanders, both staffs took steps to consult each other in order to make their work thoroughly compatible. When both commanders had signed, the letter order or directive was to be hand-carried to units and agencies for execution, and a signed copy was exchanged between the two staffs for records.

Long-range plans were subject to more elaborate procedures. An initial step consisted of a letter order or directive signed by the Chairman of the JGS and the Commander of USMACV, directing the formation of a combined working committee and specifying, among other things, 1) the purpose of the committee and a detailed agenda, 2) the composition of the committee, which usually included, on the Vietnamese side, a chairman, a deputy chairman, general and special staff officers and representatives of civilian agencies or of the ARVN Corps involved in the plan, and 3) the date-time and location of the first meeting of the committee, usually at MACV headquarters or at the JGS. Before such a letter order or directive was submitted to the Chairman of the JGS and the MACV Commander for signature, its general content had already been subjected to extensive consultations and exchange of information between both staffs.

During the first meeting of the combined working committee, its co-chairmen first relayed specific guidance instructions given by the Chairman of the JGS and the MACV Commander, then introduced their staff members by name and rank. If the plan needed extensive study and elaboration, then the co-chairmen would direct the formation of parallel US and RVN sub-Committees whose chairmen were usually counterpart staff division chiefs. Each sub-committee was responsible for the study of certain areas pertaining to its assigned staff duties. Sub-committee chairmen were assisted by general and special staff officers and if required, by representatives of GVN civilian agencies or US Field Forces and ARVN Corps. The working committee co-chairmen also determined the time allotted to staff studies and the deadline for completion. Work locations of sub-committees, however, were left to the choice of their chairmen. Then the working committee co-chairmen decided on the following meetings during which progress of sub-committee works would be reported and reviewed. The review process usually took long working sessions of the combined committee. After each sub-committee reported its progress, there were comments and lengthy discussions. The plan was gradually modified and updated until final agreement was reached by both staffs and approved by the co-chairmen who then decided on procedures for dissemination. This planning process took place between the JGS and MACV every year since late 1965. Its product was the "Combined Campaign Plan" which provided specific guidance and directives for the joint military effort to be taken up by the RVNAF and US forces during the following year. Planning work was usually started by mid-August and ended by early October. The final plan was disseminated by mid-October to ARVN Corps and US Field Forces as a basis for detailed operational planning. Operational plans were subsequently submitted by ARVN Corps and US Field Forces to the JGS and MACV respectively for approval by the end of the year.

Another major combined effort which took place each year was the RVNAF development and modernization plan. This involved force structure planning which was jointly reviewed by the JGS and MACV before being submitted to Washington for final approval.

The procedure for force structure planning usually started by a JGS recommendation, which was based on force structure increase requirements and accompanied by justifications as to manpower, organization and training capabilities. Force structure increase usually involved the formation of new units recommended separately by the services. The requirement presented by the JGS was a compilation of recommendations made by Corps and the services with the concurrence of their advisers. Combined staff meetings between the JGS and MACV were then called, during which the JGS presented its requirements and justified them. After the justifications were deemed satisfactory, the JGS would send a formal request to MACV under the form of a force structure plan. The plan was reviewed and modified as necessary by MACV, which then formally notified the JGS of every modification made to the original request. MACV notification served as basis both for the JGS to develop implementing programs and for the Ministry of Defense to plan its budget for the following fiscal year. A schedule was finally established by J-3, JGS, for the activation and training of units in coordination with the Central Logistic Command which was responsible for the timely issue of equipment for the new units. During the implementation, every difficulty which arose unexpectedly was jointly solved by the JGS and MACV. In brief, the RVNAF development and modernization plan was subjected to very close coordination between the JGS and MACV throughout its whole process, from initial planning to the final employment of new units.

Operational Coordination

The JGS and MACV were not responsible for organizing and conducting tactical operations. Their role was to monitor, supervise and support operations initiated and conducted by ARVN Corps and US Field Forces. As a result, the bulk of staff work performed by the JGS and MACV in operational matters focused on technical and support problems.

As usual, based on joint assessment of the situation, the JGS and MACV advised commanders of ARVN Corps and US Field Forces of the military efforts to be conducted in their areas of responsibility, which generally fell into two major categories: search and destroy, and pacification support. The JGS and MACV also advised them of additional support resources they might expect to receive and how long and where these resources would be provided.

These advices were given to Corps and Field Forces commanders in several forms, the most usual of which were: 1) messages, 2) confidential directives, and 3) general operational concept. Upon reception of these advices and based on them, ARVN Corps or Field Force commanders established operational plans for their areas of responsibility. These plans were usually presented by the field commander in person to the Chairman of the JGS or the MACV commander. As far as ARVN Corps were concerned, each plan was often accompanied by requests for support or troop reinforcements. If an operational plan was approved, its support requirements were immediately met by the JGS if they lay within RVNAF capabilities. In case these requirements were beyond RVNAF capabilities, an arrangement would be made with MACV to obtain the support from US resources.

Firepower support requests usually involved additional US tactical air or B-52 strikes which were allotted by MACV on a priority basis. For tactical movements ARVN units were reinforced as required by VNAF airlift assets if the operation involved the displacement of heavy equipment. Most of the times, however, they had to rely on their own assets. If the movement required a concentrated use of helicopters, the JGS would take steps to make them available by reassigning VNAF assets from other Corps Tactical Zones for the duration of the operation. In such cases, MACV would provide helicopter support for the CTZ whose assets had been temporarily reassigned. In most combined operations, additional helicopter support for ARVN troop movements was usually provided by MACV or US Field Forces. The JGS met a Corps request for troop reinforcement in a particular operation by redeploying reserves from another, or other Corps when the general reserve was not available. In those cases, arrangement was made with MACV to provide a US emergency reaction force for the Corps whose reserves had been redeployed.

On the US side, operation plans presented by Field Force commanders for their areas of responsibility (CTZ) were studied and reviewed by MACV staff division chiefs before submitting them for discussions in a joint session with their JGS counterparts. As soon as an agreement was reached on operational support requirements, both staffs would present the plan for approval by the Chairman of the JGS and the MACV commander with specific recommendations. In case these recommendations were approved, a message or directive would be issued to both Corps and Field Force for execution.

Most combined operations were subjected to approval by the JGS and MACV in keeping with the procedure mentioned above. The 1970 cross-border operation into Cambodia and Lam Son 719 operation into lower Laos were outstanding examples of combined planning effort. In a few cases, however, operational planning was entirely done by the US Field Forces involved with little participation by the counterpart ARVN Corps staff and never submitted to the JGS for discussion. The JGS operational staff, for example, knew absolutely nothing about Operation JUNCTION CITY until it was launched, although the operation plan had been published by II FFORCEV a month in advance.[2] It was learned, however, that strict security measures were enforced to prevent compromise and the planning group was held to a minimum even within II Field Force. It was doubtful then that III ARVN Corps had advance knowledge about this operation at all despite the fact that the mission assigned the planners of II Field Force read: "on order, II FFORCEV in coordination and cooperation with the III ARVN Corps conducts a major offensive into War Zone C, etc."[3]

Once a major combined operation was launched in any CTZ, it was the responsibility of both the JGS and MACV to monitor its progress and take actions to provide support as required for the duration of the operation. This was a continuous task demanding the constant updating of the situation in progress for both staffs had to keep the Chairman of the JGS and the MACV commander continually informed. As far as the JGS was concerned, the instrument that provided this continuous flow of operational data was the Joint Operations Center (JOC), which, linked

---

[2] Lieutenant General Bernard William Rogers, <u>Cedar Falls - Junction City: A Turning Point</u>, (DA, Washington, D.C.: 1974), p 85.

[3] Ibid., p 87.

together with Tactical Operations Centers (TOC) at Corps, Division and Sector levels, formed a highly integrated and instant system of operational reporting.

The Joint Operations Center was placed under direct control of the Assistant Chief of Staff J-3, JGS, and consisted of three major divisions: Operations and Intelligence, Air and Naval support, Service and Combat Arms. *(Chart 2)* To each division was assigned a US liaison officer whose duties were to channel to MACV any information not made available through the US system.

Organization, Joint Operations Center, JGS
Chart 2

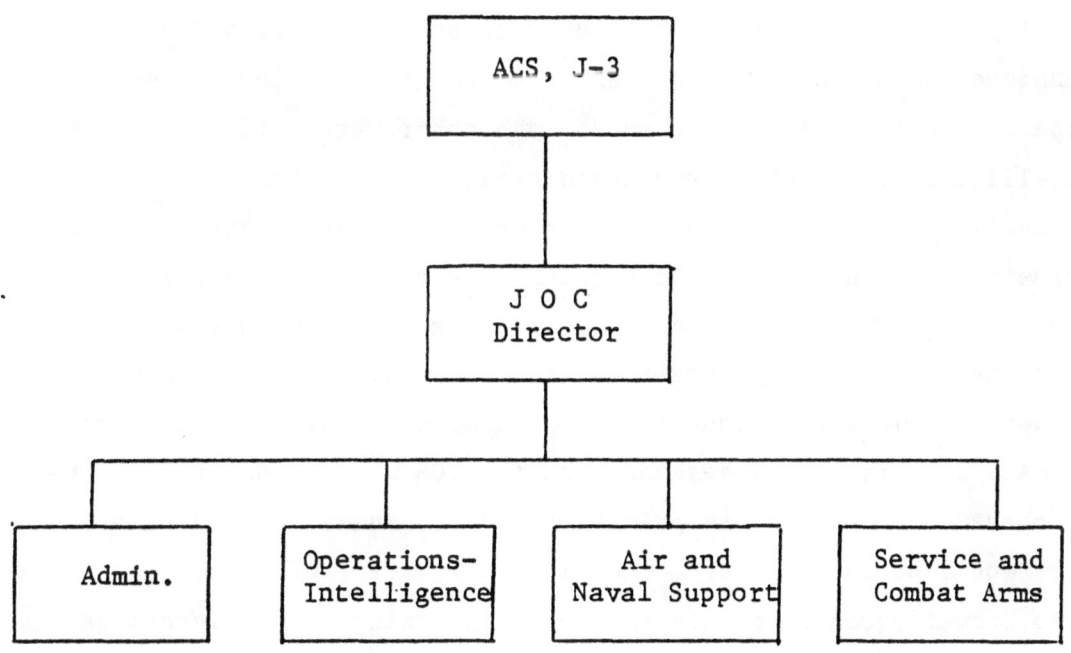

Upon completion of the operation, both the JGS and MACV were required to compile data based on unit reports in order to draw up "Operational Reports, Lessons Learned" for the benefit of future operations. If the enemy made use of any new weapon or equipment, or tactic, a combined study would be immediately initiated and the technical data as well as data on counteracting measures or techniques would be disseminated to all units.

Combined Intelligence Activities

Among the various areas of operational cooperation and coordination, none was more concrete and more successful than intelligence. This was because the combined intelligence effort was characterized by mutual support and had a common objective. Both American intelligence and its Vietnamese counterpart had its own strengths and weaknesses. The US was endowed with superior technology, sophisticated gadgets, abundant resources and a vast, competent organization, but lacked profound knowledge about the enemy. In contrast, the RVN had none of the US material advantages, but it enjoyed a vast, intimate knowledge about the enemy, his pyschology, his technique and his culture and language. So the two intelligence counterpart organizations complemented each other very well.

Intelligence cooperation and coordination between the JGS and MACV was also solidly cemented by formal bilateral agreements which provided procedures for smooth operation and guidelines for problem-solving. It was agreed, for example, that enemy captured weapons, in general, would belong to the party who happened to seize them, but as far as sophisticated weapons and equipment were concerned, the item captured would be turned over to MACV for test and assessment and the JGS would benefit from the results obtained. As to enemy prisoners and returnees, it was agreed that they would be turned over to the RVN as a matter of principle. There were also formal agreements such as those concerning signal intelligence and photo intelligence for example, which both the JGS and MACV precluded from disseminating to third countries if such intelligence was collected outside the RVN. In sum, these agreements provided for a harmonious and productive cooperation that lasted throughout the years of US participation in the war.

There were in general two forms of intelligence cooperation and coordination. At the JGS and MACV level, such effort was more of a professional partnership than the advisory relationship which usually characterized cooperation at Corps and lower levels. In particular, coordination between J-2/JGS and J-2/MACV was daily effected through the intermediary of a group of US officers who operated a liaison office at J-2/JGS. Truly professional cooperation, however, was performed through weekly intelligence briefings during which JGS and MACV intelligence staffs exchanged current information and estimates on enemy capabilities in the week to follow. JGS and MACV Assistant Chiefs of Staff for Intelligence did not meet on a regular basis. They met only when it was required and the subjects of discussion between them were generally administrative in nature; they seldom discussed the enemy situation. As a result, the exchange of information concerning the enemy was rather slow and frequently outdated. Cooperation and coordination, therefore, appeared to have fallen short of their real goal which was to meet mutual information requirements. As of 1969, however, intelligence cooperation between the JGS and MACV began to function more effectively.

There were four combined intelligence agencies which performed all the functions required for the indexing, storage, interpretation, analysis, production and dissemination of intelligence. These were: The Combined Intelligence Center, Vietnam (CICV), The Combined Document Exploitation Center (CDEC), Combined Military Interrogation Center (CMIC), and the Combined Materiel Exploitation Center (CMEC). They were truly combined organizations in which Vietnamese and American personnel were paired off in almost all functions, worked in the same location and shared the same facilities. Each national element was under the control of a separate director; thus each combined intelligence agency had two chiefs at every level of organization. There were some differences, however, between American and Vietnamese elements of the same agency. The organization of each element was not exactly the same and US personnel were usually more numerous than their Vietnamese counterparts.

1. <u>The Combined Intelligence Center, Vietnam (CICV)</u>

Activated in January 1967, CICV was assigned the mission of preparing and maintaining an all-source intelligence data base for use by the JGS and/or MACV and producing and disseminating intelligence which was required by other agencies. Major functions performed by CICV included:

a. Provision of intelligence derived from, and concerned with, land form, geology, soils, vegetation, drainage, climate, lines of communication routes and avenues of approach, and man-made features.

b. Propagation of order of battle intelligence on Viet Cong and North Vietnamese Army forces in the RVN.

c. Preparation of imagery interpretations for the production of intelligence in the form of bomb damage assessments, enemy defense overlays, lines of communication studies, detailed interpretation reports and other special studies.

d. Development of targets for maximum utilization of aerial bombardment and other offensive action.

e. Formulation of technical intelligence concerning enemy capabilities, vulnerabilities, and order of battle.

To carry out its mission and functions, CICV was organized into six sections: Terrain, Order of Battle, Imagery Interpretation, Technical Intelligence, Targets, and Research and Analysis. The Vietnamese CICV organization did not include Technical Intelligence and Research Analysis because these functions were performed by CMEC and J-2 respectively. One of the technological innovations made available by US resources was the use of computers for the storage and retrieval of intelligence data.

Among the functions performed by CICV, the most important was enemy order of battle, which included enemy forces in North Vietnam, Laos, Cambodia and South Vietnam, his infiltrations and his political infrastructure in South Vietnam. By common agreement between the JGS and MACV, enemy units were categorized as: main force, local force and guerrilla. Main force units were defined as those directly subordinate to the Central Office of South Vietnam (COSVN) or an enemy military region, subregion or front. Local force units were those directly subordinate to province and district party committees and normally operating within the territorial jurisdiction of their control headquarters.

Guerrillas were defined as those fighting forces directly subordinate to the party apparatus at village and hamlet level.

A distinction, however, was made between North Vietnamese Army (NVA) and Viet Cong (VC) main and local force units. MACV defined NVA units as those formed, trained, and composed completely or primarily of North Vietnamese, in contrast with VC units which were those formed and trained in South Vietnam and whose original composition consisted primarily of people residing in South Vietnam. This distinction became unclear in time because VC units were gradually replenished with North Vietnamese infiltrated troops and ultimately were composed primarily of North Vietnamese. The enemy 5th, 7th and 9th Divisions for example, had more than 70% of their strength made up by North Vietnamese troops, and the JGS classified them accordingly as NVA units while MACV continued to consider them as VC units. The last category of enemy personnel was the Vietnamese Communist Infrastructure (VCI) which was the political and administration organization through which the Viet Cong exercised control over the people in South Vietnam. Defined as such, the VCI did not include members of the enemy military forces although guerrillas were usually an integral part of the VC infrastructure. The methods of determining enemy forces and strength also differed somewhat between the JGS and MACV. American methods were generally rigid, and MACV seldom recorded an enemy unit unless it was confirmed by two different sources. Vietnamese methods, meanwhile, were more flexible, sometimes accepting a sole source as indicative enough if no other sources were available. There arose, as a result, a discrepancy between American and Vietnamese estimates of enemy strength despite the daily cooperation and coordination.

Another area of productive combined effort made by CICV was intelligence on terrain. Two important data base documents prepared by CICV, a dictionary of geographical names and an analytical study of geographical areas, proved to be extremely valuable. Thanks to abundant aerial photo assets provided by US forces, the updating of maps and lines of communication status became faster and more accurate. CICV studies also included an analysis of rice growing areas and of the control of rice in government-controlled and enemy-held areas, which were of great value to the government of the RVN.

The largest section of CICV was Imagery Interpretation. While on the JGS side, imagery interpretation was primarily confined to aerial photos, US imagery interpretation also included infra-red photos and side-looking airborne radar (SLAR) in addition to aerial photos. Imagery interpretation was greatly enhanced by the availability of modern American facilities such as a view computer, rear projection viewer, and photo printer. Aerial photos provided by USAF units were an intelligence source most appreciated and widely used in briefings and debriefings. They were valuable in locating enemy artillery positions and were instrumental in eliminating 130-mm and 122-mm guns which shelled Hue city in June 1972.

The target section provided target data for tactical and strategic air bombardments. This was a function concerned primarily with, and performed mostly by, the US element since it involved only the employment of US Air Force units. The ARVN element confined itself to monitoring the progress, particularly B-52 sorties. It focused its effort primarily on enemy bases, sanctuaries and infiltration routes. Here again, it benefited immensely from US scientific capabilities by using the US-devised method of pattern activity analysis, which combined and synthetized as many as 30 different kinds of data on a single target. The data were recorded on eight separate overlays placed on the same area base map, and when combined and corroborated, provided a pattern which clearly indicated enemy force disposition, capabilities and probable course of action. This target area analysis technique was most appreciated by Vietnamese field unit commanders.

2. The Combined Document Exploitation Center (CDEC)

CDEC was activated in October 1965 and was designed to provide intelligence based on the exploitation of enemy-captured documents. Its functional organization included four branches: Operation, Evaluation, Translation, Storage and Retrieval. Like other combined intelligence agencies, CDEC was composed of an American and a Vietnamese element whose personnel worked together in every branch, except translation. The US element provided and operated this facility, which was capable of translating French, Chinese, Cambodian and Japanese in addition to English and Vietnamese.

The exploitation of enemy documents, which had been a major handicap of the JGS for many years because of the lack of modern copying, storage and retrieval facilities, now was greatly enhanced thanks to US-supplied modern facilities such as microfilms and xerox machines. About 10% of enemy-captured documents contained information of intelligence value. In the exploitation process, American and Vietnamese elements worked separately but exchanged final interpretation results. These results were frequently not similar. The American element relied mostly on Vietnamese civilian employees who were not usually competent in intelligence work. Enemy documents were also difficult to read since they were mostly handwritten, highly condensed, and often making use of abbreviations. In such cases, only the most experienced Vietnamese intelligence officers could read accurately and interpret correctly enemy documents.

The majority of enemy documents were captured by US forces since during the early years of US participation, it was they who conducted search-and-destroy operations against enemy bases. US forces were also trained to be document-conscious while Vietnamese troops took enemy documents rather lightly and usually discarded them in favor of weapons. This poor habit fortunately was corrected in time and the JGS was able to collect an important amount of enemy documents over the years. These proved to be extremely valuable since enemy strategy and long-range plans were known largely through the exploitation of documents. Document-based intelligence also was one of the most abundant, accurate and reliable sources.

3. <u>The Combined Military Interrogation Center (CMIC)</u>

CMIC was activated in January 1967 with the mission of interrogating enemy prisoners of war and selected returnees of importance. CMIC comprised an American and a Vietnamese element which were organized differently. The US element was organized into an Operations Branch and a Support Branch. The Operations Branch performed CMIC essential functions which consisted of interrogation, source procurement and requirement. US interrogators were usually assigned interpreters and special aids or assistance. Information obtained went into preparation of interrogation reports which were translated into Vietnamese for intra-center use. The US element also translated reports produced by the ARVN element selected for reproduction as CMIC intelligence reports and disseminated to US intelligence consumers. The ARVN element consisted of an Operation, an Exploitation and an Editing Branch. The exploitation branch performed the actual interrogation of PWs and returnees while the Editorial Branch was responsible for the preparation, reproduction, and dissemination of ARVN interrogation reports.

CMIC was capable of handling up to 63 sources. Prisoners of war usually underwent initial interrogation at tactical units before being processed to CMIC. The time of detention at the center was usually less than two months, after which prisoners were transferred either to other intelligence agencies or to detention camps. A priority system was established whereby a source was assigned first to the interrogation element to whose needs the source was considered of particular value. The results obtained by US interrogators were usually compared with and completed by those obtained by Vietnamese interrogators who enjoyed a superior knowledge of the enemy language and psychology and could more effectively detect any fabrication, false or inflated deposition made by the prisoners. Treatment of enemy prisoners at CMIC was considered good as attested to by visits and reports made by the International Red Cross.

It was this humane treatment which earned the trust and full cooperation of captured enemy personnel. Vietnamese interrogators were trained to use psychological methods in order to obtain better results. Punishment or torture were almost never used. Detained enemy personnel were given the opportunity to observe CMIC activities and draw conclusions for themselves. An enemy provincial political commissar, for example, decided to cooperate with our interrogators after realizing that what happened to him was not what he had been educated to believe. What struck him the most was the absence of torture and the free, democratic way of life among ARVN officers and enlisted men. Another high-ranking returnee, who was a Southerner regroupee, was completely dismayed when his family was brought to him for a visit. In general, information provided by enemy prisoners of war and returnees proved highly valuable, no matter what rank they held. It was a frequent error on our part to attach value only to rank and position, because the Communist education system enabled even the lowliest cadre to have a fairly good knowledge of the tactics as well as the strategy to be employed in a certain military campaign.

4. <u>The Combined Materiel Exploitation Center (CMEC)</u>

Among the four combined intelligence agencies, CMEC was the last to be established. Its mission was to examine, evaluate, and classify captured enemy materiel and to prepare and disseminate technical intelligence reports, summaries and analyses. CMEC also provided "Go Teams" to respond to requests from tactical units or for exploitation of other targets of opportunity which could not be processed in a normal manner.

Enemy materiel was classified into 5 categories: Communications-Electronics, Weapons and Munitions, Medical, Mobility, and General Supplies and Equipment. CMEC did not possess an elaborate laboratory system for the test and analysis of all types of materiel. On the Vietnamese side, enemy materiel was usually routed to related services for examination and evaluation. The same applied to the US element which usually shipped the most modern and sophisticated enemy materiel to the US for test and evaluation. The most useful service performed by CMEC was the publication of catalogues on enemy weapons, munitions, equipment and supplies employed or to be employed in Vietnam, which helped units to identify and report newly captured materiel. Another CMEC valuable service was the dissemination of detailed information concerning enemy tanks and armored vehicles, and in particular, their vulnerable spots. This was instrumental in the destruction of great numbers of enemy tanks during the 1972 summer offensive.

Other modern enemy weapons processed by CMEC included the heat-seeking, SA-7 antiair missile, all captured samples of which were turned over to US forces, and the wire-guided AT-3 antitank missile. In particular, captured equipment related to cryptography were all directly routed to the US 509th Radio Research Group for exploitation. In general, technical intelligence was one of the areas in which Vietnamese had to rely entirely on American capabilities. The lack of trained specialists and the absence of a test laboratory were the major drawbacks of CMEC, as far as the JGS was concerned.

Logistical Support of the RVNAF

The RVNAF and US forces fighting the war in South Vietnam had their own logistical system and were generally self-supporting. There was, as a result, no combined logistical agency as was the case with intelligence, either at the central echelon or in the field, to provide direct support for units of both forces. Since materiel and equipment were separately managed, the principle set forth for the support of the RVNAF was maximum utilization of Vietnamese assets. Lateral coordination with the US logistical system was made only when RVNAF assets were exhausted. Provisions of additional equipment and supplies for the RVNAF were made on the basis of reimbursement.

The organization for coordination and cooperation in logistical support was in effect a parallel structure at every echelon. *(Map 1).*

US Forces	RVNAF
MACV	JGS/Central Logistics Command
US Army, Vietnam (USARV)	Central Logistics Command
1st Log. Command	Central Logistics Command
Support Command, Da Nang	1st Area Logistical Command
Support Command, Qui Nhon	2d Area Logistical Command
Support Command, Cam Ranh	5th Area Logistical Command
Support Command, Saigon	3d Area Logistical Command
Support Group, Support-Activity	ARVN service and technical units

At the central echelon, the Central Logistic Command (CLC) at the JGS was responsible for coordination with MACV J-4 in the following areas: 1) Review of TOE's and TO's for RVNAF units and agencies, 2) Estimates of major item requirements, based on TOE's, annual force structure, on hand and due-in quantities and losses and maintenance float estimates, 3) preparation of military aid budget and national budget requirements, 4) Establishment of import schedules for major items of equipment based on unit activation time-tables and other requirements, 5) Establishment of supply requisitions, 6) Management of military aid budget and national

MAP 1. — DEPLOYMENT OF MAJOR LOGISTICAL COMMANDS

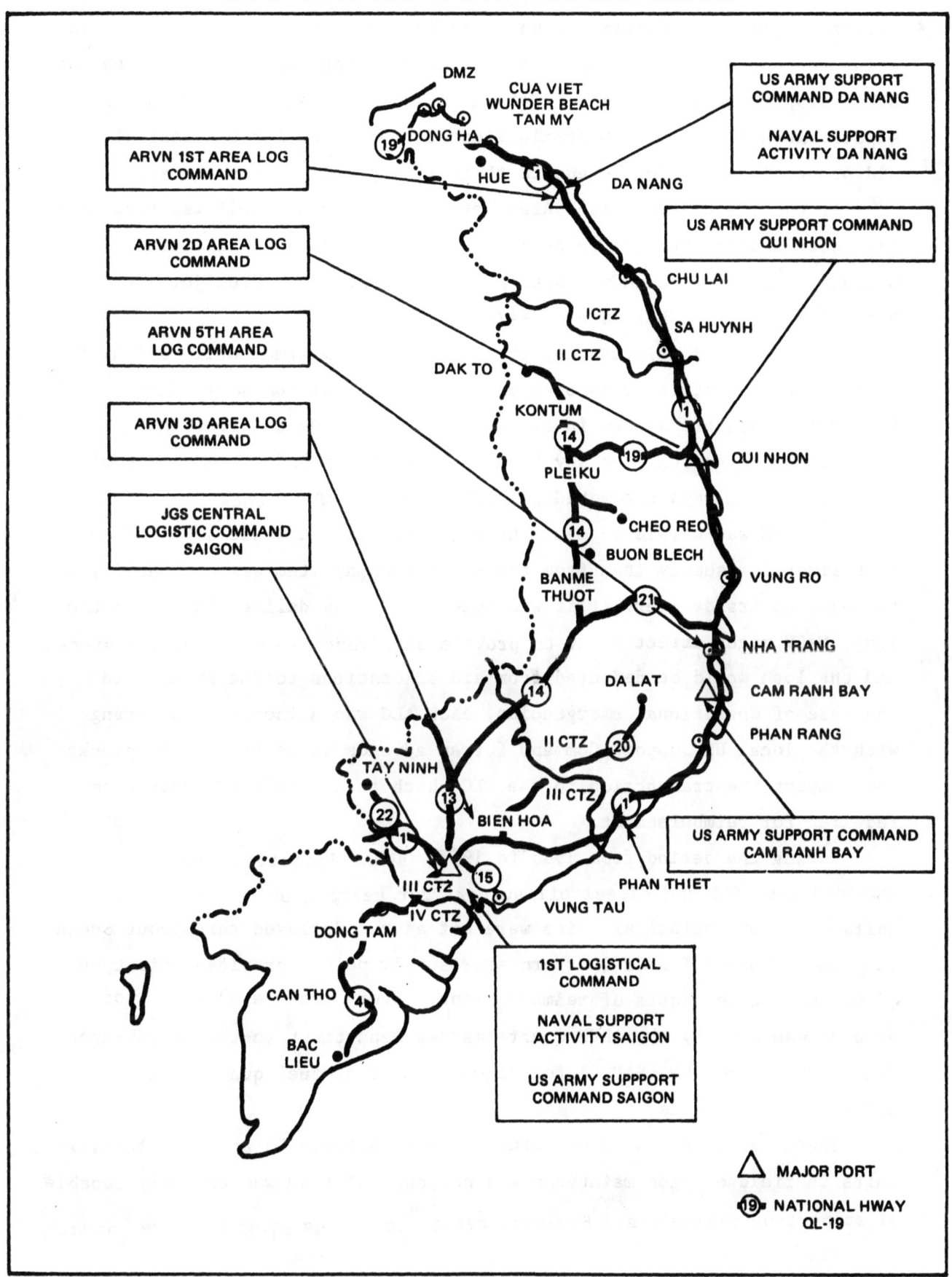

military budget, 7) Determination of logistical force structure, organization and operation procedures in keeping with national resources and the RVNAF support requirements, 8) Determination of procedures for mutual support in all areas, 9) Determination of procedures for the control of aid properties in order to ensure their timely and economical use.

At the field level, each Area Logistical Command (ALC) was responsible for coordination with the related USA Support Command in all areas of mutual support in accordance with principles and procedures jointly established by the CLC/JGS and J-4/MACV.

In supply and maintenance, the principle of maximum utilization of ARVN assets was strictly enforced. Area Logistical Commands usually relied on available stocks in field depots for issue to troop units. If there was a shortage of any kind, a requisition had to be placed with the CLC which always attempted to fill it out of ARVN stocks. In case the CLC was unable to meet the requirements, it would ask MACV J-4 to deliver the supply item from the US if such an item was not due-in, or to speed up its delivery if it was due-in. If the delivery time was too long, MACV might direct USARV to provide an advance loan out of its stocks and the loan would be deducted from aid allocations to the RVNAF. In the case of operational emergencies, each ALC was authorized to arrange with the local US Support Command for an advance issue out of its stocks then report the transaction to the CLC which then initiated procedures required for reimbursement.

During the period from 1965 to 1967, RVNAF logistical units provided gasoline and diesel oil support for certain US combat units since US logistical units were not as yet deployed throughout South Vietnam. Class III ARVN Quartermaster supply points provided this type of support on the basis of reimbursement. Every month a statement of account was sent by the ARVN Quartermaster Department to the US Sub-area Petroleum Office, VN (SAPOV) for reimbursement of fuel quantities delivered to US units.

There was practically no mutual support between US and ARVN logistical units in field echelon maintenance since each of them was entirely capable of supporting themselves. However, depot rebuilding programs were annually established by service departments in coordination with US advisers.

Transportation was one of the weakest areas in the RVNAF logistical system, and this was an area where maximum support was provided by US forces in South Vietnam. At the central level, CLC coordinated inter-regional movement and transportation requirements with MACV Traffic Management Agency and with the Military Sea Transportation Service Office, Saigon. At the field level, this coordination was performed between the ALC and the US Regional Traffic Management Agency and USA Support Command.

In port activities, it was agreed that the management and operation of South Vietnam ports, such as Saigon, Cam Ranh, Qui Nhon and Da Nang would be a US responsibility since port requirements and facilities were predominantly American. US port operation provided support for both Vietnamese civilian port authorities and the RVNAF Transportation Terminals. All goods shipped to South Vietnam, including munitions, were unloaded and transferred to Vietnamese depots by US forces.

Transportation of fuels from overseas into South Vietnam or from the storage plant at Nha Be to ports at Can Tho, Nha Trang, Qui Nhon and Da Nang was performed by SAPOV with US Naval ships or contracted commercial ships. Once shipped to the ports of destination, the fuels would be pumped directly into the nearest ARVN or US field depot, or the regional storage facilities of one of the three foreign oil companies operating in Vietnam (Esso, Shell, and Caltex). ARVN field depots then took delivery of fuels from these storage facilities to replenish depot stocks and those of ARVN-operated supply points.

Medical treatment of wounded ARVN personnel was normally performed by the ARVN Medical Service. US forces also accepted them for treatment at field hospitals if they were emergency cases brought over by the medevac system and upon requests of the ARVN Medical Service. Such treatment at US medical facilities was entirely free. US forces also provided substantial support for the RVNAF in medical evacuation by helicopters since ARVN facilities were in short supply. Requests for helicopter medevac were generally routed through ARVN operational channels. If these requirements could not be met by Vietnamese assets, then ARVN field commanders could directly request assistance from US

Field Forces. Wounded ARVN soldiers were evacuated, as a rule, to the nearest medical treatment facility regardless of who operated it.

In real estate, it was the RVN which was responsible to provide for the needs of US and allied forces, in accordance with the 1950 Pentalateral Agreement (the US, Vietnam, France, Laos and Cambodia were signatories). A GVN inter-ministerial committee chaired by the CLC commander was designated with the duties to: 1) coordinate with local authorities for the provision of land and buildings for US and allied forces, 2) determine procedures for property control, 3) review compensation rates recommended by local authorities, and 4) resolve complaints.

MACV was the sole agency which coordinated with the committee on real estate requirements generated by US or allied forces. Land was usually provided to US and Allied forces on a temporary basis and it was MACV responsibility to return it to the committee when it was no longer required. All compensations for requisitioned lands were financed by the RVN national budget. Other US requirements in buildings and storage facilities which the committee was unable to meet were fulfilled by MACV through leasing or construction.

In summary, logistical coordination and cooperation between US forces and the RVNAF brought about excellent results. The RVNAF obtained adequate support from US forces in addition to regular military aid. One of the backlashes of this generosity was the over-dependence of Vietnamese consumers on this unlimited support and a certain prejudice against the Vietnamese logistical system. ARVN unit commanders, for example, usually turned to American units nearby to obtain quick and abundant supplies of artillery munitions, grenades, fuel, and construction and barrier material, instead of requisitioning through the normal ARVN supply channel. This practice resulted in two drawbacks. First, ARVN units developed a spendthrift habit, making wasteful use of available supplies. Second, the ARVN logistical system was unable to record true requirement experiences. An outstanding example was the consumption experience pertaining to 105-ammunition. Experiences recorded during the period from 1967 to 1969 showed a consumption rate of only 12-16 rounds per day. This rate shot up to 28-32 rounds per day during the period from 1970 to 1971. When an investigation was made into firing logs, it was found that the consumption rate was the same for both periods. The balance, of course, was provided by US units whose records were unknown to the RVNAF logistical system. It's no wonder that no complaints were ever heard about shortages in munitions and other supplies during the period of US participation in Vietnam.

CHAPTER III

ARVN Corps and US Field Forces

Deployment of RVN and US Forces

When the US initiated its buildup of combat units, South Vietnam was militarily organized into four Corps Tactical Zones (CTZ) and the Capital Military Region (CMR) for the purposes of command, administration, and logistics.[1] Each Corps Tactical Zone was placed under the command of a Corps Commander who also assumed the administrative and political duties of a Government Delegate. Similarly, the Capital Military Region commander was also Military Governor of Saigon - Gia Dinh.

The 1st CTZ comprised the five northernmost provinces of South Vietnam; its northern boundary was separated from North Vietnam by the Demilitarized Zone (DMZ). The 2d CTZ encompassed twelve provinces of the Central Highlands and the coastal area. This was the largest and most sparsely populated zone. The 3d CTZ covered ten provinces surrounding Saigon and was considered the most important. The 4th CTZ was made up of sixteen provinces of the Mekong Delta, the rice bowl of South Vietnam. The CMR comprised the metropolitan area of Saigon - Cholon and Gia Dinh province whose districts surrounded Saigon like a cocoon.

Each Corps Tactical Zone was in its turn divided into Division Tactical Areas (DTA), each DTA being the tactical area of responsibility assigned to an Infantry Division. There were, as a matter of fact, as many DTA's as there were Infantry Divisions. In addition to DTA's

---

[1] In 1970, the designation Corps Tactical Zone was changed into Military Regions (MR), and the Capital Military Region became Capital Military District (CMD), under operational control of MR-3. DTA's were abolished (Presidential Decree No. 614a-TT/SL of 1 July 1970).

a Corps Tactical Zone might include a Special Zone assigned to a separate subordinate command, such as the 24th Special Zone of the 2d CTZ which was responsible for Kontum and Pleiku provinces. Each DTA encompassed several provinces which, under the military territorial organization system, were called Sectors. In most cases, the province chief, usually a field-grade army officer, was also Sector Commander.

In addition to a civilian administrative staff, each province had a Sector Command which was responsible for the tactical employment of Regional and Popular Forces (RF and PF) to assure territorial security for the province. Operationally although not administratively, provinces or Sectors were under control of the DTA of which they were part. The Sector's area of responsibility or province was further divided into several Subsectors or Districts. Subsector commands were the lowest military control bodies of the military territorial organization system.[2] Depending on its size, each sector might include from two to eight subsectors. *(Chart 3)*

Tactically, infantry divisions were assigned to CTZ's as a general function of population density, enemy strength and the level of enemy activities in each zone. Thus the 3d and 4th CTZ, which by far controlled the majority of the population, were assigned three infantry divisions each. All four CTZ's, in principle, were placed under operational control of the Joint General Staff (JGS). Due to the nature and proportions of the war, which was mostly fought at the division level and rarely at Corps level, corps commanders were delegated authority for operation planning and execution under the supervision of the JGS.

In view of the severe enemy pressure in South Vietnam, the build-up of US and other combat forces of the Free World Military Assistance Organization (FWMAO) was effected rather rapidly. By March 1966, US Field Forces had been deployed throughout the country. At that time the aggregate

---

[2] At the end of 1973, a lower echelon of military territorial organization, the Sub-subsector, was created at the village level. Its functions were to assist the village chief in controlling and coordinating village security forces to incude National Police, Popular Force, and People's Self-Defense Force (PSDF). This organization was proved highly effective in neutralizing enemy infrastructure.

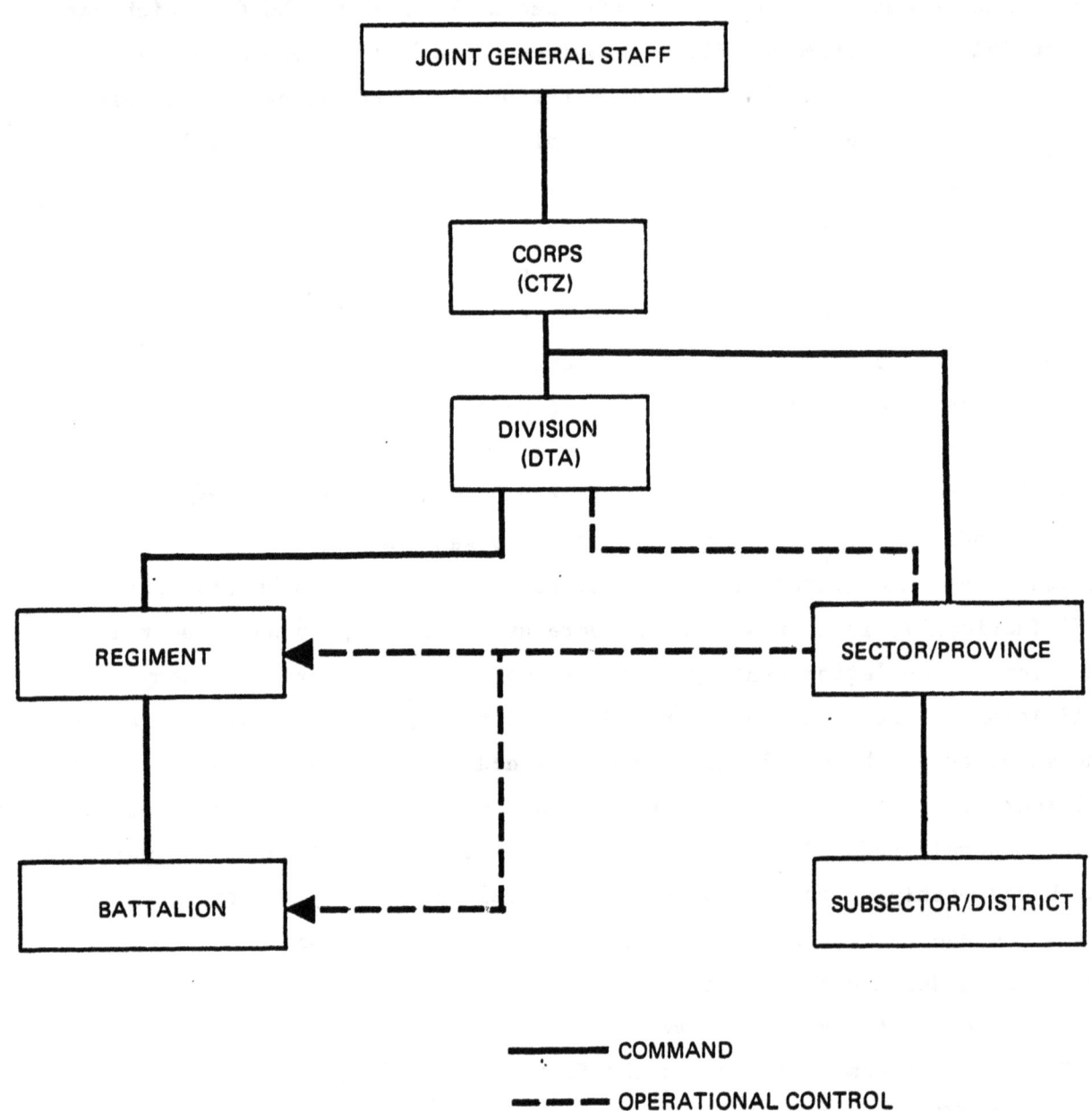

CHART 3—RVN TERRITORIAL COMMAND AND CONTROL

strength of the Republic of Vietnam Armed Forces (RVNAF), US, and FWMA forces stood at 816,000 men, including 581,000 of the RVNAF, 22,400 of the FWMAF, and 213,000 of the US forces. The FWMAF represented contributions made by the Republic of Korea, Thailand, Australia, New Zealand, the Republic of China, and the Philippines, in decreasing order of importance.

During this period of US buildup, the RVNAF force structure was made up of: 1) Regular Forces; Army, 273,000; Navy, 15,000; Air Force, 13,000; Marines, 7,100; 2) Territorial Forces: Regional 135,000; Popular, 137,000, or a total of 580,000 men under arms.

The Army of the Republic of Vietnam (ARVN) was composed primarily of ten infantry divisions deployed to all four CTZ's.[3] The 1st and 2d Infantry Divisions were deployed to the 1st CTZ; the 22d and 23d Infantry Divisions to the 2d CTZ; the 5th, 10th, and 25th to the 3d CTZ; and the 7th, 9th, and 21st Infantry Divisions to the 4th CTZ.[4] In addition to infantry divisions and separate regiments which were all under operational control of Corps, there were twenty Ranger battalions which were usually employed as Corps reserves, and assigned to them accordingly. An Airborne Division and a Marine Division constituted the General Reserve under direct control of the JGS. In total, there were 141 maneuver battalions of the RVN regular forces operating throughout South Vietnam.

The Regional and Popular Forces assumed responsibilities for territorial security at province, district, village and hamlet levels. The Regional Forces were basically organized into companies assigned to provinces.[5]

---

[3] The total number of ARVN infantry divisions increased to 11 when the 3d Infantry Division was activated in October 1971 to replace the US 3d Marine Division.

[4] In 1967, upon recommendation of the 10th Division Commander, Brigadier General Do Ke Giai, who believed that number 10 was a bad number, the 10th Division was changed into the 18th, presumably a luckier number.

[5] In 1970, RF Companies were consolidated into battalions; later on, in 1974, RF battalions were grouped into Mobile Groups with organic artillery support (one battery of four 105-mm howitzers).

There were, in addition, 12 RF battalions. RF companies operated within the confines of a province and under the control of the province chief/sector commander. Popular Forces were organized into platoons. Lightly armed, PF platoons assured the protection and security of villages and hamlets where they lived, under the control of the district chief/subsector commander. As a rule of thumb, each PF platoon was assigned to a hamlet.

Free World Military Assistance combat forces included: the 1st Battalion Royal Australian Regiment, and a 105-mm howitzer battery of the Royal New Zealand Artillery, totalling about 1,400 men and operating in the 3d CTZ under operational control of the US 173d Airborne Brigade (Separate); and the Republic of Korea forces which were mainly deployed in the 2d CTZ and comprised the "Capital" Infantry Division and the 2d Marine Brigade, with an aggregate strength of over 20,000 men. In total there were 10 maneuver battalions of the FWMAF in South Vietnam.

During this period of time, US combat force structure in South Vietnam was made up of: 1) Air Force, 28,747 men; Marines, 39,441 men; Army, 134,324 men; Navy 10,111, and Coast Guard, 462 men.

US tactical air support was provided by the US 2d Air Division. The mission assigned this division was to defend the airspace of South Vietnam, maintain air superiority, conduct operations to destroy enemy units, and provide air-ground support as required.

The US III Marine Amphibious Force (MAF) which included the US 3d Marine Division and the 1st Marine Air Wing, and other supporting units, was deployed in the 1st CTZ. Total III MAF combat strength was made up of 13 maneuver battalions operating in the five northern provinces which were the Marines' assigned tactical area of operation.

US Army units made up the bulk of US combat forces in South Vietnam. During this period of time, US Army units included: the 1st Air Cavalry Division (Air Mobile), the 1st Brigade, 101st Airborne Division, and the 3d Brigade, 25th Infantry Division, operating in the 2d CTZ; the 1st Infantry Division, the 173d Airborne Brigade (Separate), and the 2d Brigade, 25th Infantry Division, assigned to operate in the 3d CTZ. However, there were no US combat units deployed to the Mekong Delta.

In total, there were 28 US maneuver battalions operating in the 2d and 3d CTZ. *(Map 2)*

In general, despite their heavy logistical appendages, US units were deployed where tactical requirements warranted their commitment, particularly units that enjoyed great mobility such as the Air Cavalry Division and the Airborne Brigades. In contrast to ARVN infantry divisions, no US unit was made responsible for a permanent tactical area of responsibility.

The deployment of US forces throughout South Vietnam—except the Mekong Delta—brought about the most reasonable balance feasible between friendly and enemy forces. There were, in each Corps Tactical Zone, sufficient forces for the protection of important population centers and enough combat strength to conduct sweep operations. The build-up of US and FWMA forces also raised the morale of ARVN troops and restored confidence among the population.

Organizational Arrangements for Command and Control

Following the accelerated buildup of US combat troops, command and control organizations were also rapidly developed and by March 1966, US field commands were already in place throughout the country. It was from this time on that large-scale offensive operations began and initiative was gradually regained on all battlefields.

To exercise command and control over US forces in the field, General William C. Westmoreland, Commander, USMACV, instituted in each Corps Tactical Zone—except the 4th CTZ— a US Field Force Command. There were:

1. The III Marine Amphibious Force (III MAF) command, activated in May 1965, and co-located in Da Nang with Headquarters, I Corps, RVNAF. III MAF was responsible for military operations in the 1st CTZ.[6]

---

[6] Initially, III MAF was called III Marine Expeditionary Force. The term "Expeditionary" was later dropped because it was unpopular among the Vietnamese who still recalled with bitter resentment the French Expeditionary Corps. "Force" was also favored over "Corps" because this term had been used for the RVNAF; besides, it was confusing sense to have two Corps in the same CTZ.

MAP 2. — DEPLOYMENT OF MAJOR ARVN AND US UNITS, MARCH 1966

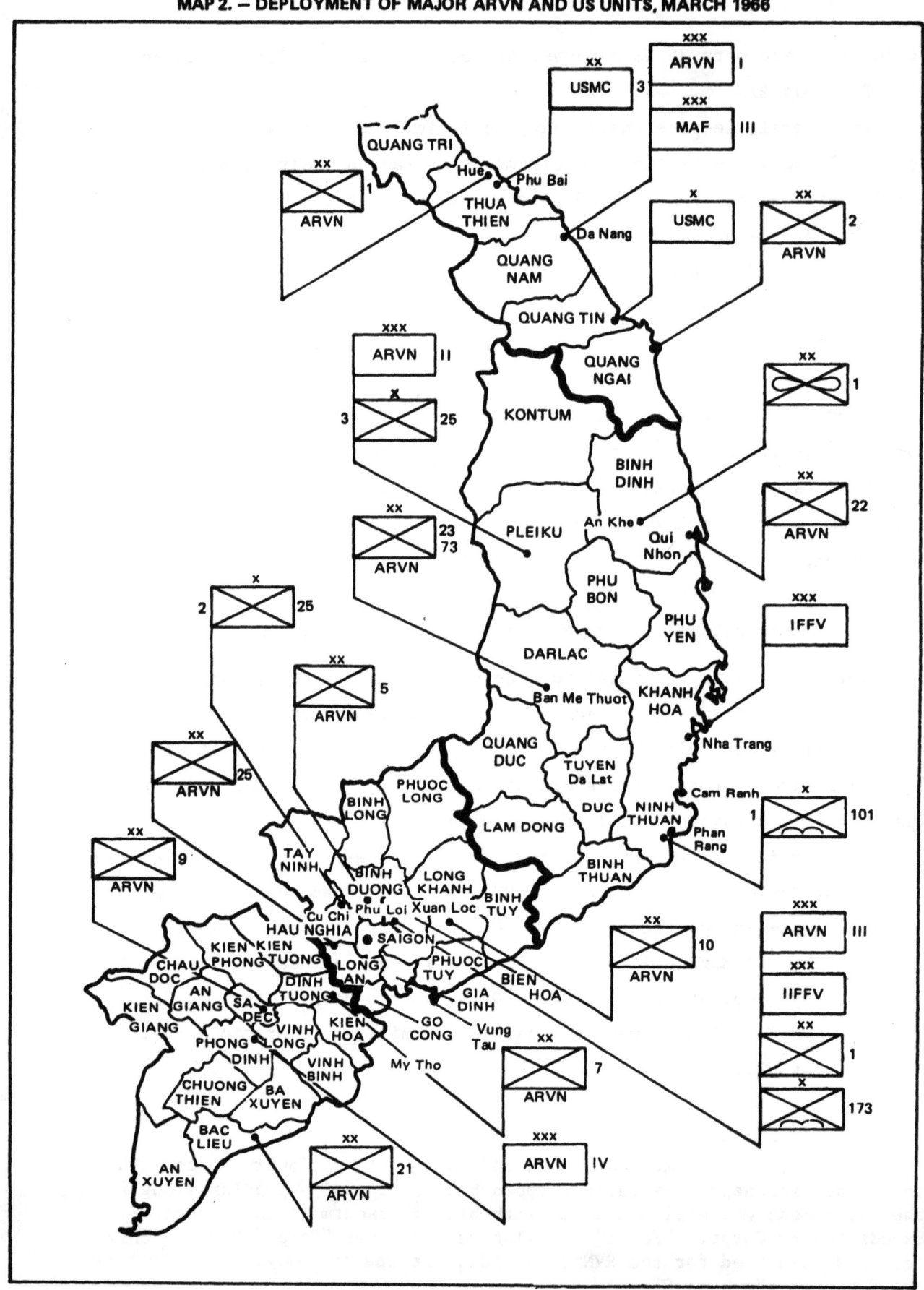

2. The I Field Force, Vietnam (IFFV) Command, activated as of September 1965 and located in Nha Trang. IFFV was responsible for military operations in the 2d CTZ. II Corps Headquarters, however, was located in Pleiku.

3. The II Field Force, Vietnam (IIFFV) Command, activated in March 1966, and co-located in Bien Hoa with Headquarters, III Corps, RVNAF. IIFFV was responsible for military operations in the 3d CTZ and the CMR.

The functions of a US Field Force Command were essentially the same as those of an ARVN corps command, which involved primarily the operational control of combat and combat support units assigned to it, with the exception that, unlike the ARVN Corps, the US Field Force was not strictly bound by territorial duties. The collocation of III MAF and II FFV Headquarters with those of I and III Corps respectively, made cooperation and coordination between US and RVN forces easier and more convenient. The physical separation in the case of I FFV and II Corps was offset to some extent by instant and extensive communications, and by frequent staff and command visits.

The organizational concept behind Field Forces was a sound one. It befitted the political and military situation of that time by preventing the confusion of having two corps operating in the same area of responsibility on the one hand, and by providing flexibility for the span of control, which could be easily adjusted to changing tactical requirements and command responsibility, on the other.

In early 1968, to counteract the severe threat caused by the presence of NVA units in the two northern provinces of the 1st CTZ, the Commander, USMACV, decided to reinforce this area with two additional US units: the combat-proven 1st Air Cavalry Division and 101st Airborne Division. At the same time, MACV Forward was activated and installed in the Hue - Phu Bai area, under the command of General Creighton W. Abrams, Deputy Commander MACV, to exercise supervision over increasing combat and logistics activities of US Air Force, Naval, Army, and Marine units in the area. A month later, MACV Forward was deactivated and transformed into US Provisional Corps, Vietnam, under the command of Lt. General William B. Rosson. Later still, Provisional Corps, Vietnam was changed into US Army XXIV Corps as of August 12, 1968. XXIV Corps exercised operational control over all US forces operating in the area defined by the DMZ in the north, and by the Hai Van Pass, just north of Da Nang, in the south. These forces included the 3d Marine Division, the 101st Airborne Division, the 1st Air Cavalry Division, and the 1st Brigade, 5th Infantry Division (Mechanized). XXIV Corps also closely coordinated combat operations with the ARVN 1st Infantry Division in this area. (Chart 4)

Also, during 1968, tactical expediency in the face of the enemy Tet offensive led to the creation of an additional field command whose components were drawn from the II FFV. Called "Hurricane Forward," this field command was collocated with the CMD and exercised control over US forces operating in the Saigon - Gia Dinh area. As of June 4, 1968, however, this temporary field command took on a permanent character and became the Capital Military Assistance Command (CMAC), under Major General John H. Hay. CMAC planned for and operated the defense of the Saigon - Gia Dinh area in coordination with commanders of the US 7th Air Force and Naval Forces, Vietnam, and the Saigon - Gia Dinh Military Governor, Major General Nguyen Van Minh.

The final development of US command and control structure in South Vietnam included the activation of the Delta Military Assistance Command (DMAC) on April 8, 1969, whose commander, Major General George S. Eckhardt, was also senior adviser to the commander, IV Corps. DMAC was created for the express purpose of controlling US forces which operated separately in the Mekong Delta, including the US 9th Infantry Division (-).

The aforementioned field commands continued operation until 1970 when they began to decrease in strength or downgrade along with the gradual redeployment of US and FWMA forces from South Vietnam, and the turnover of combat responsibility to the RVNAF.[7]

---

[7]On March 9, 1970, XXIV Corps Headquarters moved to Da Nang to take over III MAF. Lt. General Melvin Zais, Commander, XXIV Corps became senior adviser to the I Corps Commander.

CHART 4–ARRANGEMENT FOR COMBINED COMMAND AND CONTROL, ICTZ

(APRIL 1968)

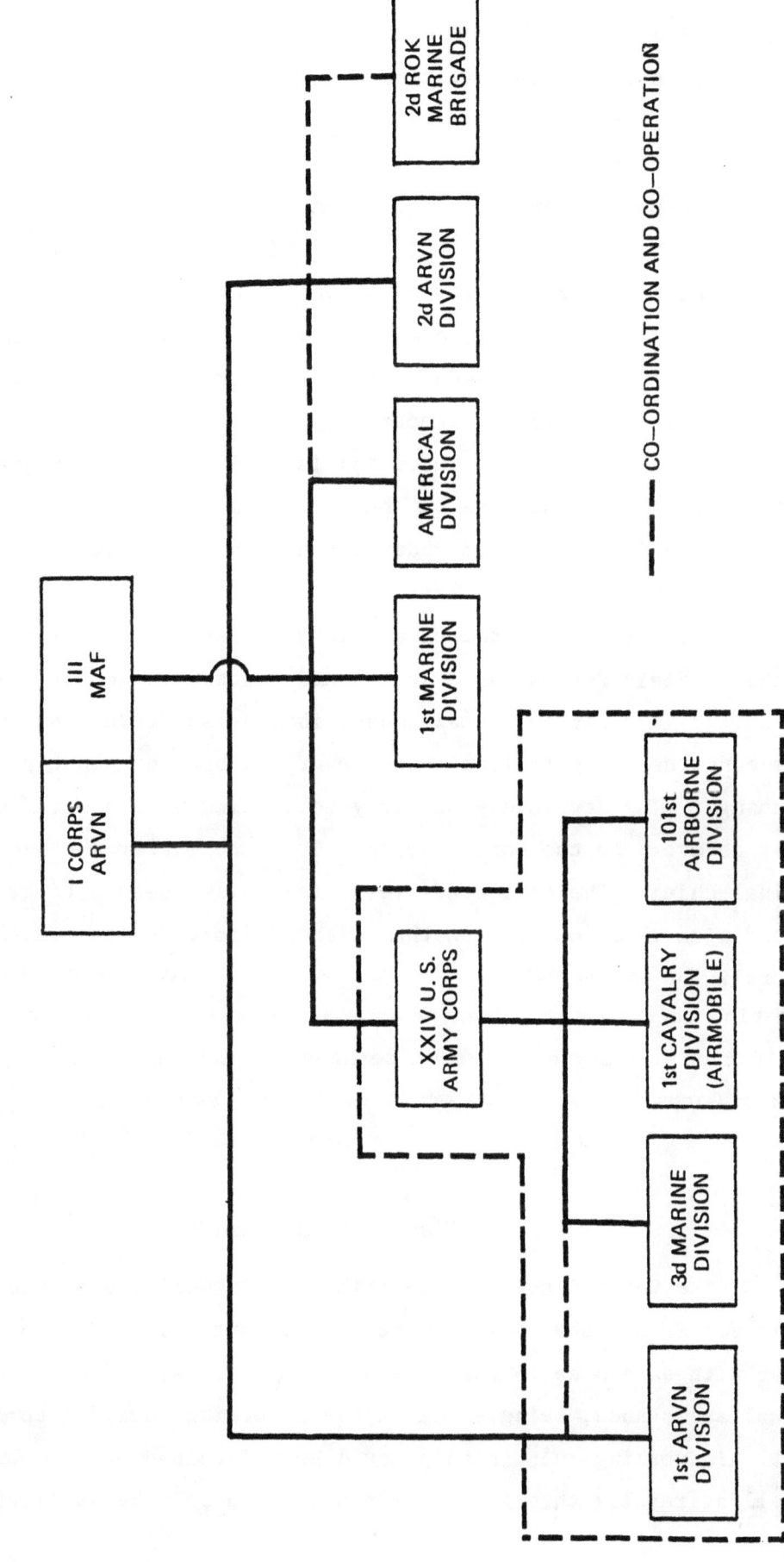

With the introduction of US ground combat forces in South Vietnam, and following the activation of US Field Force commands in all four Corps Tactical Zones, some modification in the US advisory effort became necessary. When he first arrived in Da Nang, the commander of the US III MAF was designated as senior adviser to the commander of I Corps. Consequently, all I Corps US advisers were placed under operational control of the commander, III MAF. The former US senior adviser, a colonel, now became deputy senior adviser. The same arrangement was applied to the 2d and 3d CTZ when I and II FFV were activated. The two former senior advisers to II and III Corps also became deputy senior advisers under the commanders of I and II FFV, respectively, who became senior advisers. The case of the 4th CTZ was an exception in that there were no major US units operating in the area at that time. As a result, the US advisory organization in the 4th CTZ underwent no change and continued under direct control of MACV. *(Chart 5)*

The realignment of the US advisory system in view of the presence of the US Field Forces was a shrewd and suave arrangement which paid off handsomely in a psychological sense, insofar as Vietnamese commanders were concerned. Operationally, however, it brought about practically no change. The day-to-day advisory activities were carried on as dutifully as ever by the Corps Advisory Group no matter who became the nominal chief. The senior advisers, meanwhile, seemed to be more concerned with their own troops than with advisory duties, which was perfectly natural. In retrospect, if the US Field Force Commander could have given more time to his role of senior adviser,—i.e., cooperation and coordination on a daily basis—then perhaps the combined military effort in each Corps Tactical Zone would have been much better.

Mission Relationships

At the Corps Tactical Zone (Military Region) level, the three US Field Forces and their Vietnamese counterparts, the ARVN Corps, were on a par with each other. They operated on the basis of cooperation and mutual assistance, being equal partners working toward a common goal. That this working relationship could be maintained and bring about excellent results throughout the years could only be ascribed to a

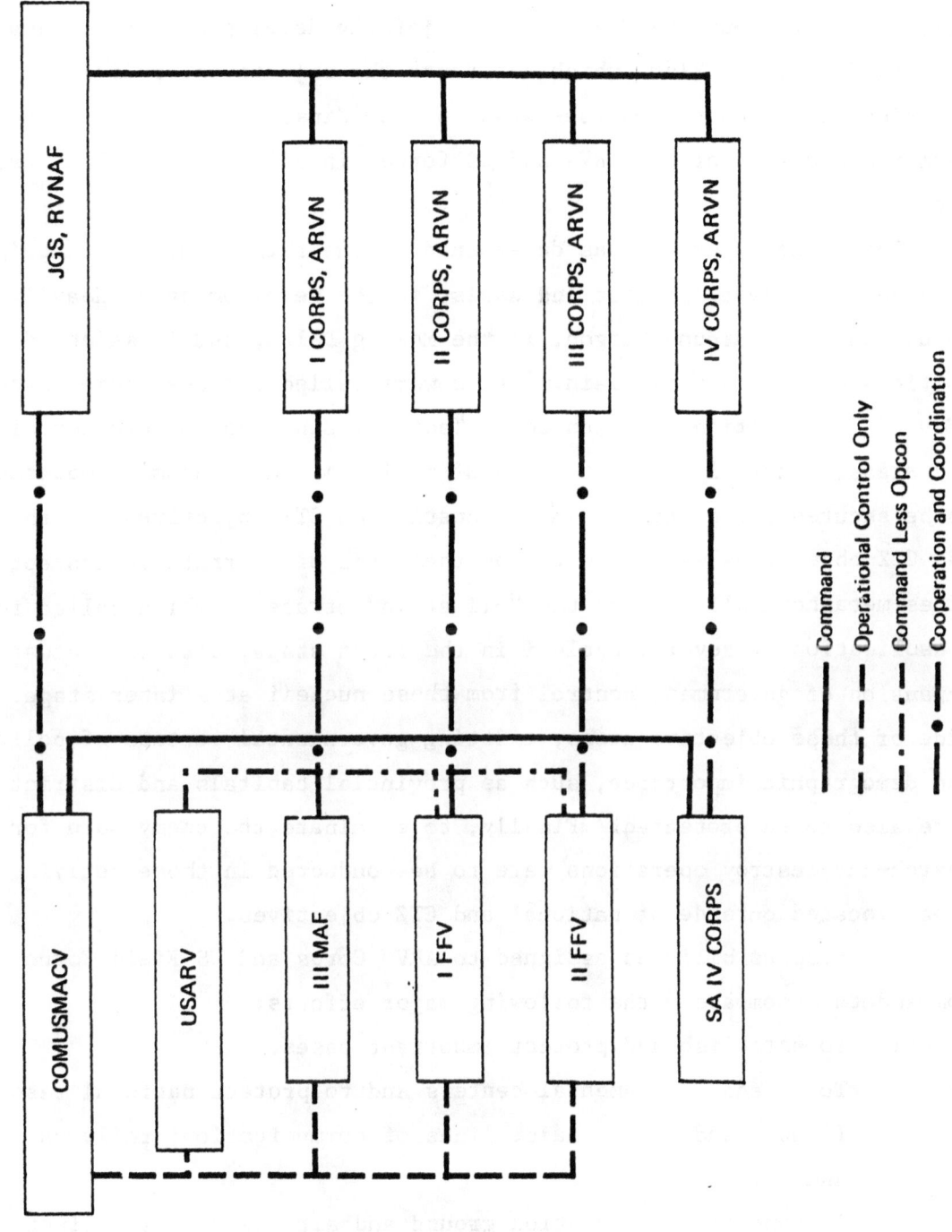

CHART 5—COMMAND RELATIONSHIPS

commendable spirit of willingness and self-effacement on the part of the field commanders involved.

Beginning with 1966, with a view to expand and coordinate offensive military operations, MACV and the JGS jointly developed a comprehensive "Combined Campaign Plan" which set forth the objectives, policies, relationships, and the various areas of coordination required for a harmonious effort of both RVN and US forces in all the Corps Tactical Zones.

The basic objectives as determined by the first Combined Campaign plan were to clear, protect and assist in the development of heavily populated areas around Saigon, in the Mekong Delta, and in selected portions of the coastal plain. These were called national objectives. *(Map 3)* In addition, in each Corps Tactical Zone, there were certain key areas, generally populated and of political and economic importance, to be secured and protected which constituted CTZ objectives. Both national and CTZ objectives were selected on the basis of a strategic concept—sometimes metaphorically called the "oil stain" strategy—which called for the consolidation of several nucleii in the first stage, then the outward expansion of government control from these nucleii at a later stage. Outside of these objective areas, existing governmental centers of political and demographic importance, such as provincial capitals and district towns, were also to be protected. Finally, to eliminate the enemy main force, search-and-destroy operations were to be conducted in those outlying areas located outside of national and CTZ objectives.

The responsibilities assigned to ARVN Corps and US Field Force commanders encompassed the following major efforts:

1. To establish and protect important bases.
2. To defend governmental centers and to protect national resources.
3. To open and secure major lines of communication, railways and waterways.
4. To conduct long duration ground and air operations against enemy forces and bases.
5. To neutralize the enemy strategy.
6. To provide security for the expansion of government control.

MAP 3. — 1966 COMBINED CAMPAIGN OBJECTIVES

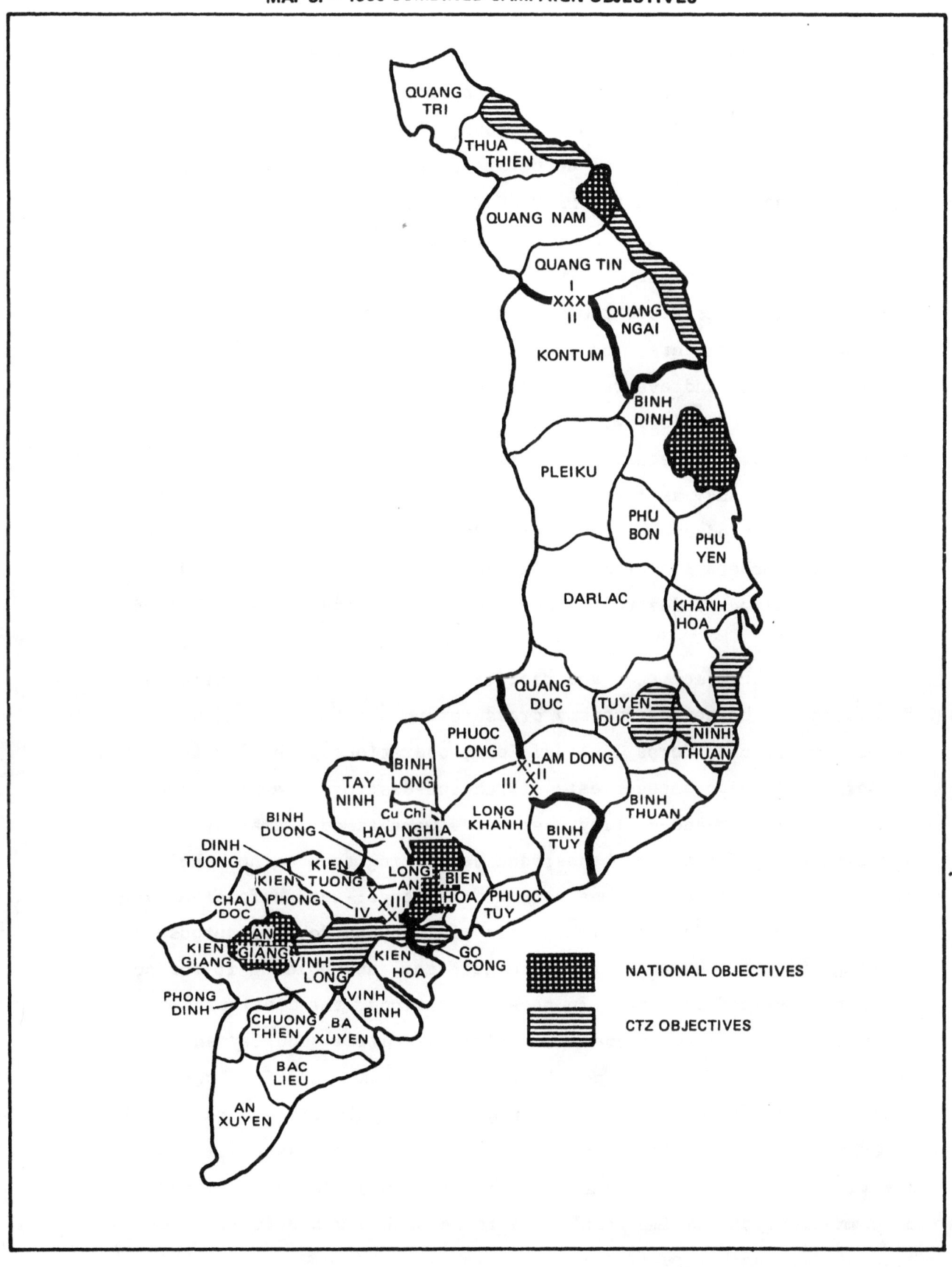

7. To interdict land and sea infiltration routes.

8. To provide tactical air and logistic support.

Under the guidelines thus provided, ARVN and US field commanders in each CTZ were directed to cooperate with each other to conduct operations based both on the MACV-JGS-established operational schedule and on the requirements of assigned responsibilities and the situation in the Corps Tactical Zone. The basic operational concept during that period of time prescribed the employment of RVN forces for the protection of governmental centers, the protection and control of rice and salt producing areas, and eventually for sweep and secure operations in selected areas of priority. US and FWMA forces, meanwhile, were responsible for the security of their bases, the clearing of areas adjacent to those bases and, as directed, assisting in the defense and control of rice and salt producing areas. In addition, Vietnamese, US, and FWMA forces, in cooperation with one another, would conduct offensive-type operations aimed at destroying enemy units and bases located beyond secure areas.

Despite the fact that the tactical aspect of the situation varied according to the periodic enemy pressure and the terrain and weather of each particular Corps Tactical Zone, operations generally fell into one of three major categories: search-and-destroy, clearing, and securing. Search-and-destroy operations were aimed primarily at locating enemy forces and bases, and destroying them without holding terrain. Clearing operations were of the longer-term offensive type conducted in coordination with territorial forces for the purpose of driving enemy forces away from a target area, and holding it for an indefinite period of time. In these operations, the continuing presence of friendly forces was deemed necessary to provide security and instill confidence among the local population. Securing operations were generally conducted by territorial forces, frequently augmented by a regular ARVN or US reaction force if necessary. They were mostly saturation patrolling activities conducted on a permanent basis to provide security for lines of communication and important localities within a particular Tactical Area of Responsibility (TAOR).

In keeping with the above directives and policy, large-unit offensive operations, at brigade and higher level, were conducted on a regular basis—mostly by US forces and on their initiative—in all CTZs, except the Mekong Delta. With abundant firepower and mobility, US units usually focused their efforts in searching out and destroying major enemy units and logistical bases, or reacted in response to the situation and intelligence recorded. The RVNAF, meanwhile, were stretched over the entire national territory for which they were responsible. With only limited firepower and mobility, Vietnamese units usually operated in populated areas near the major axes of communications, and concentrated their primary effort on the support of pacification and rural development.

Combined operations which integrated or paired off ARVN and US units were sometimes conducted, depending on the tactical situation or as a response to the force requirement of certain types of effort, provided that both sides could muster enough forces for the operation.

In the 1st CTZ, for example, after it was discovered that the NVA 324B Division had infiltrated into an area north of Cam Lo (Quang Tri) in late June 1966—the first instance of a NVA division recorded crossing the DMZ—operation HASTINGS/LAM SON 217 was launched. It was a major combined operation conducted by the ARVN 1st Infantry Division reinforced by general reserve units and the reinforced US 3d Marine Division. During the operation which lasted from 7 July to 3 August 1968, friendly forces clashed violently with NVA forces from the moment the operation was launched until it was terminated. The enemy 324B Division suffered considerable losses in this operation.

In the 2d CTZ, the US 1st Air Cavalry Division, joined by Vietnamese and South Korean units launched several consecutive operations to clear the coastal plain in northern Binh Dinh which was a national objective. The operations, code-named MASHER/WHITEWING/THAN PHONG II, lasted from January 24 to March 6, 1966 and succeeded in destroying the major part of enemy regional main force units in the area, and at the same time inflicting heavy losses on the NVA 3d (Gold Star) Division.

Another large scale combined operation, ATTLEBORO, was conducted from September 14 to November 24, 1966, with the participation of the US 196th Light Infantry Brigade, the US 1st Infantry Division, the 3d Brigade, US 4th Infantry Division, the US 25th Infantry Division, and the US 173d Airborne Brigade, combined with forces of the ARVN 5th Infantry Division. It was the largest combined operation until that time striking into the enemy War Zone C in the 3d CTZ. The operation inflicted severe losses on the enemy CT-9 Division and 101st Regiment, drove them across the Cambodian border, and resulted in large quantities of weapons, ammunition, and supplies being captured. The enemy winter (dry season) campaign plan in Tay Ninh province was thus thwarted.

The joint military effort, made during the initial stage of US participation, resulted in several concrete achievements. Enemy forces and his combat potential were seriously attrited and his infrastructural organizations badly damaged. Due to these achievements, South Vietnam was able to overcome a most dangerous period, regain its balance and stability, enlarge its control and restore confidence among the troops and population.

The actual accomplishment of common responsibilities depended in a large measure on the cooperation and arrangement between US and ARVN field commanders in each Corps Tactical Zone. As directed by MACV and the JGS, US Field Force and ARVN Corps commanders jointly initiated courses of action, determined the conduct of operations and assigned intermediate objectives to divisions, sectors and other subordinate units. In general the joint concept of force employment during this period tended toward assigning ARVN units more responsibility for territorial security than for mobile combat operations. Lacking substantially in combat support facilities, ARVN units were yet to prove their combat effectiveness and reliability. So the primary effort of seeking out and destroying the enemy was taken up by US forces who, in view of their substantial firepower and mobility assets, enjoyed a great tactical advantage and usually held the initiative in large-scale operations. It was assumed that for these reasons, US forces were better suited to the task of eliminating enemy main force units and destroying enemy bases which were usually located in jungle and mountain areas.

This division of tasks between US and ARVN forces no doubt spared the ARVN Corps commanders the major war burden. It was also a reflection of the prevalent political situation in which Corps commanders played a preeminent role. Still affected by an undercurrent of instability, the RVN military government found it prudent to entrust political power to Corps commanders who were selected among members of the ruling Armed Forces Council. As a result, ARVN field commanders were sometimes more preoccupied with politics than combat operations. The I Corps commander, Lieutenant General Nguyen Chanh Thi, for example, was deeply involved in politics because of the close relationship he enjoyed with military rulers. His controversial role in the Buddhist uprising in 1966, however, led to his dismissal. A Corps commander was usually assigned many positions of key importance. Lieutenant General Le Nguyen Khang, III Corps commander, for example, retained five additional positions for himself.[8] Because of these burdensome duties, Corps Commanders were hardly able to devote themselves to the military effort. Hardly if ever could they spare time to visit subordinate field units, provide them guidance, and follow up on their actions. As a direct consequence, command and control, morale, and discipline were adversely affected. This situation gradually improved after 1967 when democratic rule was established and more and more professionals were assigned to key commands and positions. Still, to ensure that the common effort would succeed as directed, US Field Force commanders usually played the preponderant role in the conduct of combat operations. As a result of this role and of their capacity as senior advisers, they exerted a certain influence on their ARVN counterparts.

---

[8] In addition to his political positions as member, National Leadership Committee and government Delegate to III Corps Tactical Zone, General Khang was also Commander, CMD, Military Governor of Saigon - Gia Dinh and Commander, Marine Division, a position he held for 12 years.

The deployment of forces, arrangement for command and control, and the assignment of common tasks to ARVN Corps and US Field Forces, in retrospect, can be said to be reasonable and conforming to the situation of South Vietnam at that time. This was truly an excellent working arrangement that eventually led to the successful accomplishment of a common goal through cooperation and mutual assistance. It was an arrangement that fully exploited the advantages and shortcomings of either side, and provided a good opportunity for ARVN units to learn in a most realistic manner all aspects of command, staff planning, and combat techniques through combined activities. In reality, however, both sides were more concerned with immediate goals and obtaining immediate results than attempting to reach for the objectives of a more distant future.

There were some US commanders who contended that, in view of the tremendous military power and superiority enjoyed by US forces, searching out and destroying enemy units hidden in outlying areas was not really a big challenge. This idea was shared by many ARVN commanders. It was true that the United States had more military might than required to win the war in South Vietnam if it had been willing to. But American policy was apparently constrained by its gradual response approach and failed to bring all US military might to bear on the war at the appropriate time.

Various programs of combined action aimed at upgrading the RVNAF combat effectiveness and complementing the effort of US forces at the same time were suggested but few were implemented. In fact, US units were somewhat chary of the complexities involved in coordination and the additional burden of providing all kinds of support for ARVN units. Only rarely did they suggest combined action. The reason for this reluctance was simple enough: US commanders had varying degrees of skepticism as to the effectiveness of ARVN units as combat companions. They apparently did not always think it worthwhile to cooperate with ARVN units although any ARVN unit, regardless of its size, could in fact make useful contributions to the fulfillment of their common tasks.

In addition, US Field Force and unit commanders, having to cope with several duties and obligations at a same time, and trying to perform them in a totally strange and complex environment, seldom demanded or advanced initiatives of their own concerning combined activities with Vietnamese units. As senior advisers, however, they felt obliged to take some interest in ARVN units. But the periodic visits they paid to their counterparts were largely courtesy calls or official tours characterized by all the pomp, civility and reserve of diplomatic encounters. Ever guarded and courteous, US commanders seldom offended their counterparts by critical remarks which could well have been beneficial for the success of a common enterprise. For the most part, therefore, US commanders stuck to their own business, leaving the day-to-day working contact to US advisers and liaison officers.

ARVN forces deployed in the CTZs were usually bound by their territorial security mission, and constrained by territorial responsibilities. This was a complex mission that finally absorbed and held back the great majority of regular army units. An adverse consequence was that, after a long period of operating from fixed positions, the combat spirit and effectiveness of a unit was greatly reduced. Once adapted to a certain familiar environment, troops tended to become careless and soft, and more disposed toward personal comfort; combat aggressiveness either decreased markedly or was completely gone. And in time, they became just another kind of territorial force.

Cooperation and coordination, as a compromise between military and political considerations, were certainly not an ideal way to prosecute a war, much less the war in Vietnam. But cooperation and coordination did work and did succeed, to some extent. It was only regrettable that it had not begun earlier. If, in the initial stage of US participation, US Field Forces commanders had initiated extensive combined action programs and taken advantage of their preeminent positions as senior advisers to demand more of their counterparts, then ARVN units would have certainly benefited more from the presence of and cooperation with US forces. Their combat effectiveness would have upgraded more quickly and more substantially. At the very least, their performance and discipline would have been much better. Finally, if US Field Force and RVN Corps commanders had had the opportunity and willingness to cooperate and coordinate on a daily basis, to see for themselves problems as they arose, and jointly decided on the spot how to solve them, then the combined effort to utilize every available asset to prosecute the war would have been more productive and more successful. These observations were substantiated by the remarkable progress achieved by the RVNAF after the 1968 Tet offensive through the years of intensive cooperation and coordination with US forces, and as a result of more determined efforts by the United States to help the RVNAF gradually take over the primary war burden.

CHAPTER IV

RVNAF — US Joint Combat Operations

Operational Cooperation and Coordination Procedures

Combined operations, involving the participation of both Vietnamese and American units, were planned and controlled by commanders at all echelons on the basis of cooperation and coordination. Beginning in 1966, for operations of all types — whether separate or combined — the coordination between RVNAF and US forces, and occasionally between operating forces and the local government, was governed by instructions provided by MACV and the JGS in the annual Combined Campaign Plan. Procedures established for such operations by MACV and JGS also applied, by extension and with some modifications, to unilateral operations.

RVN and US commanders were instructed to personally discuss planned operations as early as possible in order to arrive at an agreement on purpose, general objectives, operational concept, participating forces, and planned duration. All these provisions were laid out in written orders which served as guiding instructions for the staff and subordinate units. Following the initial agreement, commanders were to meet periodically with each other in order to review planning progress and issue further instructions as necessary.

As soon as there was agreement between commanders, staff officers of both commands convened to plan operational details. Based on guiding instructions agreed upon, the planning task was aimed at: (1) determining objectives, responsibilities, forces, phases and projected duration of the operations; (2) determining the boundaries of tactical areas of responsibility to be assigned to each force; (3) arranging details for air, artillery and naval support and other support requirements; (4) issuing guidance and instructions to subordinate commanders.

In view of security requirements both commanders implemented special measures to ensure secrecy for the planned operation, such as (1) limiting the number of planning personnel, (2) utilizing the tactical operations center or a safe working area with limited access, (3) strict control of documents and materiels used in the planning process, message transmissions, and in particular, all telephone communications pertaining to the operation.

Subordinate staffs and commanders were subsequently informed in time in order to proceed with timely planning and coordination for the operation. Appropriate security measures, again, were taken to prevent disclosure.

When the operation was about to be initiated, the US and ARVN commanders involved established their command post at the same location, usually at a Fire Support Base in order to facilitate coordination, mutual support, and common decision making. These collocated command posts were provided with adequate personnel and facilities for the coordination and control of combat support assets such as air, artillery and naval fire, engineers, and helicopters. At the Corps and Field Force level, command posts were usually not collocated, but liaison officers were exchanged between RVN and US command posts in order to assist in planning, directing and supervising the operation.

When the operation was conducted to support the pacification and development program, early coordination was made with local authorities. In the case of US forces, this coordination was effected through the US advisory teams assigned to the local government.

When operations were conducted unilaterally, US forces usually coordinated with the local government at province and district level through local US advisory teams. This coordination sometimes included the establishment of an operational liaison team at the local government headquarters. In order to allow for timely coordination, US tactical commanders were instructed to contact the local US advisory teams as early as possible.

During the operation US units made maximum use of ARVN liaison personnel with a view to facilitating coordination with and identification of friendly forces. The ARVN liaison personnel were also used to identify and make contact with the population. In addition, US tactical commanders were instructed to pay equal attention to psywar and civic-action activities in conjunction with tactical activities. United States Operations Mission (USOM) and Joint US Public Affairs Office (JUSPAO) representatives were provided to assist them in planning and implementing these activities which were also coordinated with ARVN units and the local governments in the area of operation.

When ARVN units operated independently the Vietnamese tactical unit commander was instructed to cooperate and coordinate with local authorities, and establish operational liaison with US units. He and his US adviser coordinated and established liaison with US units and local US advisers in the area of the planned operation (province or district). ARVN unit commanders were also directed to give attention to psywar and civic action activities in conjunction with combat activities. These programs and activities were to be coordinated with the local government.

A salient feature of the Vietnam war was that the civilian population usually lived and stayed in the area of operation during the course of military operations. As a result, US and ARVN forces were instructed to exercise great caution to minimize human casualties and property losses to the local population.

When contact was made with the enemy in a sparsely populated area, air and artillery fire could be applied freely in keeping with standing operating procedures. In the absence of enemy contact, however, non-observed fires were to be delivered only after targets had been cleared with local authorities, ARVN liaison officers, and artillery or air forward controllers.

The employment of naval gunfire, artillery, and tactical air on enemy-held or suspected targets in villages or hamlets that were usually inhabited by the local population was regulated as follows. These regulations applied to both US and ARVN forces.

1. All firings should be controlled by airborne or ground forward air controllers (FAC) and air or ground forward observers (FO), and should be carried out only upon approval by local authorities, and by US and ARVN units involved in the operation.

2. Even in case of being fired upon by enemy small weapons from villages or hamlets not located within the ground area of operation, the operational unit was permitted to attack only after warnings had been given by leaflets, loudspeaker broadcasts, or other appropriate means.

3. A village or hamlet may be fired on without warning if the fire support plan included such firings in support of infantry troops maneuvering through the area, or if the commander was certain that warning would be detrimental to the operational mission.

Intelligence

With the buildup of US combat forces and the extension of combat operations throughout the country, there was an urgent need for the unification of American and Vietnamese intelligence efforts. This was an area of vital interest to MACV and the JGS. At the beginning of US participation in the ground war in 1965, ARVN combat intelligence capabilities were still undeveloped. Knowledge about the enemy was scant and not subjected to systematic collection and analysis. ARVN combat intelligence came of age and became the effective instrument it was largely due to cooperation and coordination with US intelligence agencies.

A major step forward was taken by MACV and the JGS when Combined Intelligence Centers, staffed by US and RVNAF personnel, were established to operate the four key intelligence functions: interrogation of enemy prisoners, exploitation of enemy documents and materiel, and establishment of intelligence reports for both US and RVN command systems.[1] With

---

[1] See Chapter II.

technological and material support provided by the US, these Combined Intelligence Centers functioned effectively and provided accurate, timely intelligence for the combined combat effort at the highest level.

At the Corps level, intelligence cooperation and coordination was effected between ARVN Corps G-2 and the US intelligence advisory section which provided advisors for each G-2 functional component. US advisors usually provided G-2 with intelligence data collected by US sources such as aerial surveillance and photo reconnaissance, infra-red (Red Haze) photography, side looking airborne radar (SLAR), and US-controlled agents. In return, G-2 provided US intelligence advisors with intelligence data collected through Vietnamese sources, such as interrogation reports, document exploitation, and information provided by ARVN-controlled agents. The same procedure for cooperation and coordination was found at division and regimental levels. In fact, practically all direct intelligence cooperation and coordination between ARVN Corps and US Field Forces was effected through the advisory system.

ARVN liaison officers were usually attached to US combat forces operating within a Corps Tactical Zone. These ARVN liaison officers assisted in relations with local governments and with the people in the areas of operation. US combat forces, however, required immediate assistance in the exploitation of captured documents and the interrogation of prisoners of war or returnees. This assistance was provided by ARVN military intelligence (MI) detachments assigned to US forces at the Field Force or Corps, division, and separate brigade levels. Each MI detachment was initially authorized 8 officers, 18 NCOs and 4 enlisted men and organized into a headquarters, an interrogation team, a document exploitation team, an order of battle team, and an imagery interpretation team. Later, its strength was revised to 20, with 2 teams, one for interrogation and one for document exploitation. The MI detachment mission was to provide on-the-spot exploitation of intelligence data collected by US combat units for immediate reaction purpose. It was also used by US units to establish contact and liaison with local governmental authorities, RF and PF, and with the national police when they operated in populated areas. The ARVN MI detachment cooperated with its US military intelligence counterpart, which was under the operational control of the US G-2.

With modern, abundant technical facilities and efficient organization and operation, US forces could easily overcome difficulties in intelligence when they conducted operations in remote areas against enemy bases and sanctuaries. Cooperation and coordination with ARVN corps and divisions usually provided them with supplemental intelligence data for their operational purposes. When operating in populated areas or in support of RVN pacification, however, the acquisition of targets and identification of enemy personnel became a real problem. Intelligence cooperation and coordination at the territorial level, i.e. province and district, was usually a complex business because in addition to the normal tactical intelligence cooperation with ARVN units, US forces were also required to coordinate with several intelligence agencies at sector or subsector level, such as the Provincial Intelligence Coordination Committee (PICC), the Phoenix Committee, the Provincial Security Committee, the Screening Committee, etc., and not infrequently with local forces as well. An efficient procedure devised by some US units to handle this complexity was the establishment of a Combined Intelligence Center, as was the case with Fairfax operation, or a Combined Interrogation Center under the control of the US G-2 or S-2. Members of this combined interrogation center included representatives of local US and RVN intelligence agencies, such as the National Police, Special Police, Provincial Reconnaissance Unit (PRU), Police field force, Sector or District S-2, Military Police Interrogation Section and the G-2 or S-2 staff of the unit. Through this combined intelligence effort, prisoners of war, returnees, suspects, and refugees could be rapidly screened, classified and interrogated to provide instant information required for immediate action. In addition the Combined Interrogation Center also alleviated to a great extent the requirements placed on the local screening committee by serving as a clearing house for detainees of all types.

In general, the cooperation and coordination effort in intelligence between US and RVN forces was a subject of particular emphasis and mutual interest. This combined effort helped US forces overcome their initial unfamiliarity with the local environment and their relative inexperience

with regard to enemy local forces. It also enhanced ARVN intelligence
capabilities and brought about mutual faith and a healthy professional
relationship between US and RVN intelligence organization at all levels,
including combined Long Range Reconnaissance Patrols (LRRP). The exchange of information, whether through channels of the hierarchy or
laterally, was gradually improved and became swift and effective
enough to serve its purpose. Intelligence estimates produced by ARVN
Corps G-2, for example, were widely respected by both US Field Forces
and MACV. The primary weakness in the ARVN process of intelligence
collection and production, however, was the difficulty in obtaining
timely, accurate intelligence reports from subordinate units and from
sectors and subsectors; lack of trained and qualified personnel; and
lack of adequate technical intelligence resources. Also, because of the
elusive nature of the war, the acquisition of targets, which was usually
the key to operational success, was only partially effective.

Operational Planning

In many cases, planning for long-duration campaign or large-scale
operations was initiated by Americans. Vietnamese staffs usually played
only a marginal role, and their contribution was somewhat pro forma.
Vietnamese field commanders had little interest in planning. This was
because they did not control the combat support assets required, and
also, frequently, because they did not have a good grasp of the situation
involved. Most of the time the Vietnamese field commanders would only
offer a few comments on US-drafted plans or would just uncritically
approve the recommendations made by US advisers. They seldom involved
their staffs in the planning process.

In the context of the Vietnam war, ARVN corps and divisions were
also responsible for territorial security in addition to the conduct of
combat operations. Their staffs, therefore, usually worked at and controlled all activities from fixed headquarters. When tactical

requirements demanded the establishment of a Forward Command Post, which was usually done at division level, the bulk of key staff personnel still remained at the main headquarters, performing territorial duties. That explained why Vietnamese commanders called these forward CPs "light". A light CP usually consited of the unit commander and a few members of his operational staff. Thus, the limited staff personnel, who were usually inexperienced and with little training, were unable to provide the continuous planning and coordination required by intense combat operations. They were also unable to determine tactical requirements for combat and combat support. As a result, operational plans were usually not updated. Vietnamese staffs often tried to make up for these deficiencies by issuing some orders at the last minute. This created even more confusion and difficulties for the effective coordination between combat and support actions.

Tactical planning at regiment and battalion level was even more haphazard due primarily to the very small size of their staffs and the lack of experienced and knowledgeable staff officers. At these levels, staff officers usually did not know how to coordinate intelligence resources or to make effective use of combat support. Also, the general shortage of staff officers made it difficult either to direct subordinate units in daily activities or to plan for future operations. These grave deficiencies put the planning burden squarely on the unit commander's shoulders. Frequently the unit commander did most of the informal staff planning while his staff did only routine work and waited for orders. The inevitable result of all this was that US tactical advisers were compelled to assist the ARVN unit commander and sometimes to take over the entire planning task.

Generally, ARVN unit commanders at all levels made tactical decisions without a basis of formal planning. An adequate and timely operational plan was a rare thing in ARVN field units. Planning activities were generally confined to the top level, with minimal participation of staff officers and performed only on a daily basis. Partial or segmental orders, which changed with every passing day, were the usual practice for conducting operations. These orders usually allowed very little time for maneuver and support units to complete preparations. The orders were also frequently given at the very last minute. The result was confusion, loose coordination between maneuver units, and ineffective employment of combat support assets. Also, intelligence directives were seldom issued along with combat orders. Subordinate units, as a result, rarely concerned themselves with the execution of intelligence plans.

In practice such deficiencies in staff planning did not affect the operational coordination effort seriously. This was because, through US advisers, the ARVN units usually maintained lateral coordination, at every tactical level, with US units. To function effectively they depended primarily on this lateral coordination instead of directives and guidance given through the ARVN channel, which, if ever made available, merely reiterated, rather belatedly, what the unit had already learned from US advisers. And because operational coordination never ran into trouble, there appeared to be no need for combined planning, which unfortunately was seldom made a subject of common interest or concern at the tactical level.

There was no question that US units always operated according to plans which were usually detailed and timely. Planning was an American inherent forte. Not only did American field commanders have a total grasp of the tactical situation, they also enjoyed tremendous support assets. In planning, they were particularly security-minded; and because of the constant fear of leaks, they tended to do the bulk of the planning unilaterally when combined operations were to be conducted. There was, of course, the usual coordination with, and some contribution from, Vietnamese counterparts at the beginning of the planning process. However, this was apparently just a formality. By having the Vietnamese make an initial contribution, the Americans undoubtedly wanted to spare them the embarrassment of being dependent on American initiative and blindly following what had been laid out. Therefore, when the Americans departed they left behind a critical weakness in the ARVN operational command process. Now ARVN field commanders had to make do with poor planning and as a result, usually made haphazard tactical decisions which were never based on careful study and analysis.

Over the years of fighting alongside US units and working with US advisers, it was true that ARVN units had learned a lot and matured in every aspect: technique, staff work, and tactics. Cooperation and coordination did give ARVN tactical commanders excellent opportunities to develop their leadership and assume the combat responsibility. It was unfortunate, however, that once left to themselves, most of them usually reverted to their old habits, the habits they had acquired well before the advent of US-RVN cooperation. Very few of them indeed, took any interest in correcting themselves to keep abreast of new trends in warfare and to adjust to the requirements of the tactical situation. As a result, staff planning remained one of the gravest deficiencies among several ARVN field commands up to the final days.

Assignment of Objectives, Operational Areas and Free-Fire Zones

To ensure complete coordination prior to planning for a certain combined operation, both the ARVN field commander and his US counterpart ought to have advance agreement on the assignment of operational areas, free fire zones and objectives for each unit. In the context of a war without clearly defined frontlines, operational efforts usually concentrated on destroying the enemy and expanding the government-controlled area instead of pushing forward a physical frontline or occupying more enemy-held territory as is the case with conventional warfare. In keeping with this warfare aspect, Corps Tactical Zone commands usually determined the areas on which friendly efforts should be concentrated in order to provide security for the population, drive off the enemy main force units, and interdict enemy infiltrations. These areas of concentrated effort were determined on the basis of local environment, enemy activity level, the location of enemy bases, population density, lines of communication and terrain.

In general there was common agreement on four clearly-defined types of areas or zones based on the criteria mentioned above. Secure areas consisted of populous centers where the local government was well established and operating effectively. Movements were free within these areas, day and night. In such areas, there were in general no major enemy actions save for occasional sabotage or random shellings. Consolidation areas were sandwiched between secure areas and clearing zones. These areas were usually under government control and subjected to intensive pacification. In such areas, the control of resources and population were strictly enforced. Enemy actions in these areas were usually not conducted on a large scale. They were limited and took place most often in the form of shellings and sabotages. The primary responsibility of friendly forces assigned to consolidation areas was to prevent the enemy from making inroads into secure areas. Next in the security scale were clearing zones which were in effect contested areas placed under the control of field commanders. These clearing zones were usually divided into Tactical Areas of Responsibility (TAORs) assigned to combat units whose mission was to destroy enemy units and bases. Clearing zones, in general, included friendly operational bases, unpopulated areas, and areas under enemy control.

Finally, adjoining the national boundary were border surveillance zones. These were areas in which tactical unit commanders were responsible for detecting enemy troop concentrations and taking necessary security measures. Border zones were usually included in tactical areas of responsibility. *(Chart 6)*

Basically, ARVN regular forces as well as US units were assigned operational missions in clearing zones in order to stop the main force units from infiltrating into consolidation or secure areas and to assure continuous improvement of the security situation. It was in clearing zones that combat operations were usually conducted, either separately or jointly, and focused on destroying enemy main force units and logistics or operational bases. Friendly units operating in clearing zones were also tasked to provide support, whenever required, for RF and PF units

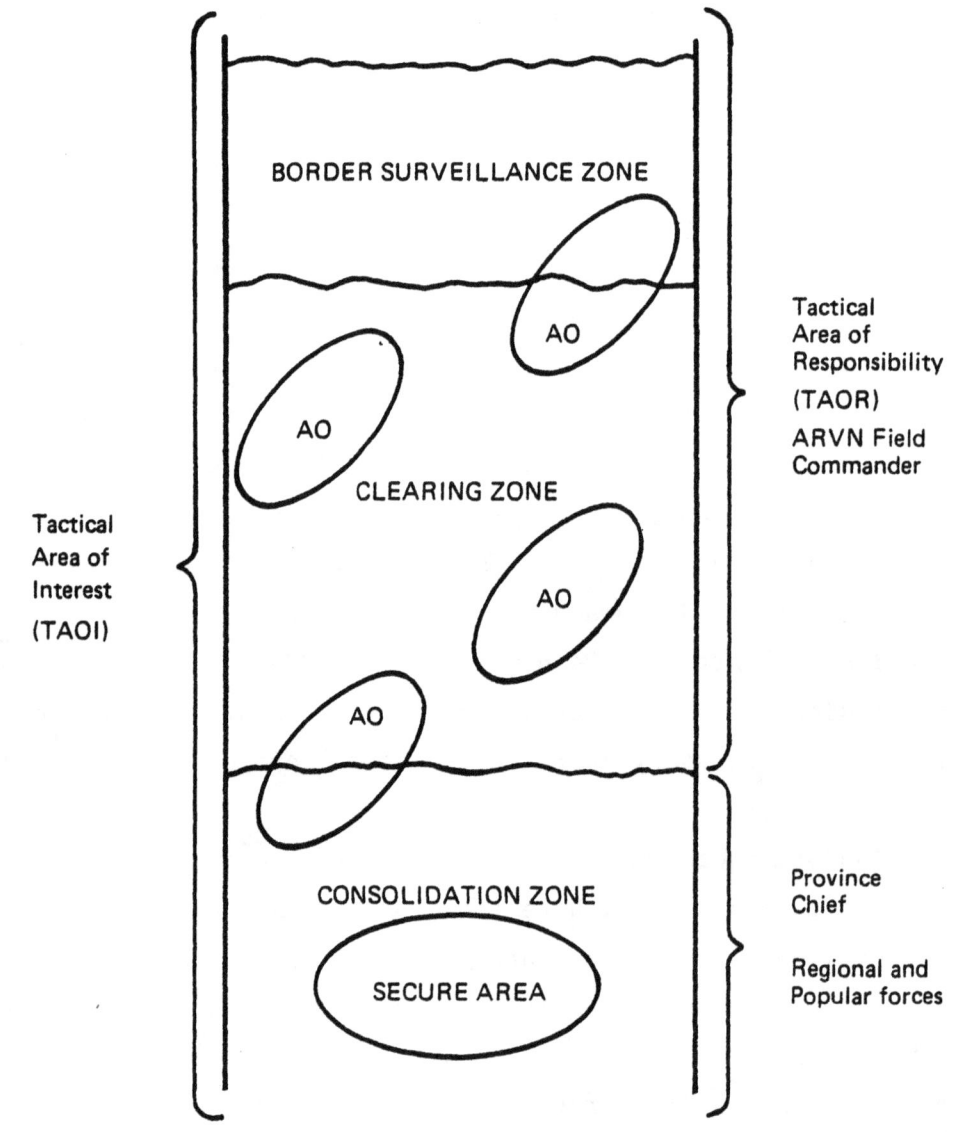

CHART 6—CONFIGURATION OF TACTICAL ZONES AND AREAS

and for other pacification forces such as PSDF, National Police, RD cadres, PRU, and armed propaganda teams. The support was to be through the destruction of enemy forces who threatened friendly local forces in the consolidation or secure areas. At the same time, border activities were conducted to interdict enemy infiltration efforts.

As a general rule, ARVN units concentrated their effort primarily on consolidation areas where the population lived and participated in pacification support whereas US units which, because of their powerful firepower and great mobility, took up a further-reaching effort, focusing primarily on unpopulated clearing zones. This division of responsibility also recognized the inherent difficulties US units experienced due to language and cultural differences. US units also provided support to friendly territorial forces by destroying those enemy forces detected in consolidation or secure areas in case ARVN units were not up to this task.

In keeping with this operational concept, ARVN Corps Tactical Zone and US Field Force command usually assigned to each division or separate brigade a Tactical Area of Interest (TAOI); each TAOI included, but was not necessarily limited to a TAOR. It was a duty of the tactical commander who was assigned a TAOI to throughly familiarize himself with the local environment, and to keep track of friendly activities in the area. Thus, through mutual cooperation and coordination, maximum effectiveness of friendly forces and firepower could be achieved. The difference between a TAOI and a TAOR lay in the fact that within a TAOI, the responsibility of a tactical commander was general in nature and not limited to tactical actions or military operations. Depending on the relationship between ARVN Corps and US Field Force commanders and the particular aspect of each Corps Tactical Zone, ARVN and US major units were assigned a common TAOI to conduct parallel or combined activities, or each unit was assigned a separate TAOI.

A division, in turn, assigned to each of its subordinate regiments or brigades a Tactical Area of Responsibility or an Area of Operation (AO). In each TAOR, the tactical commander was fully empowered to develop and maintain bases and installations, control movements and to conduct combat operations on a continuing basis with forces under his operational control.

Every fire and maneuver action taken in a particular TAOR by any friendly force had to be thoroughly coordinated with the force commander of that TAOR. Depending on the tactical situation and intelligence, a unit which was responsible for a TAOR would be assigned an Area of Operation (AO) to conduct an operation of some duration. An area of operation was assigned only to a particular operation; it might be located within or without a TAOR. Battalions or units subordinated to a regiment or brigade, in general, were not assigned permanent TAORs. They were tasked to conduct operations only to liquidate objectives within an area of operation.

There were several instances in which the enemy took advantage of the fixed boundaries between tactical areas of responsibility by conducting activities in the area straddling a common boundary or using it as a safe haven to elude friendly operations. To prevent the enemy from doing this, several measures were taken. First, friendly activities were concentrated on objectives located along boundaries. Second, a common boundary might be modified or displaced upon agreement by the responsible units concerned, depending on the tactical situation and the terrain in the area of operation. Third, there was usually advance agreement or coordination between operational commanders and adjacent territorial commanders on the conduct of operations or pursuit actions across boundaries, mutual reinforcement and support, as well as other necessary measures.

Beyond friendly areas of operation, there were zones in which firing could be freely applied. In these free-fire zones, firing, strafing, or bombing could be instantly called whenever the enemy was detected without fear of confusing him with the local population and without having to obtain time consuming clearances from local military and civilian authorities. Like interdiction coastal zones, free-fire zones were areas through which the enemy usually moved his troops and supplies or which he used as safe havens from which to launch shellings or ground attacks against friendly units. These free-fire zones were of course off-limits to the local population; and movements to and from these zones were severely limited. While the civilian population generally stayed out of these areas, there were exceptions.

Sometimes the civilian population chose to enter prohibited areas where they could find some productive farmland or a fish-yielding canal or coastal lagoon, despite the dangers that might shower on them at any given time. As a matter of fact, the local population knew that friendly control over these areas was not entirely tight or permanent, particularly at night. Consequently, the application of fire on those free-fire zones sometimes inflicted losses on the local populace. There was no way to tell, at night, whether the prowling people were enemy troops or just some fishermen taking in their catch.

Another device for facilitating operations against the enemy while avoiding harm to the civilian population was the imposition of curfews. Briefly speaking, curfews were imposed in insecure areas during the hours of darkness, generally from midnight or sometimes earlier till dawn. During this period, the friendly population was required to remain in their houses. Accordingly, any movement at night could be automatically considered inimical and engaged at once.

The only problem which arose was the imposition of over-restrictive curfew hours—almost always by an over zealous province chief—, which interfered unduly with civilian pursuits. As an area became secure, curfews were progressively relaxed and eventually lifted completely. In areas where the authorities and the people were in rapport and communicated freely, the curfew hours could be adjusted readily. In some areas, however, the curfew was a source of friction, particularly where fishermen were concerned since fishing was conducted most productively at night.

In general, free-fire zones were theoritically a sound idea. In trackless jungle, mountainous areas and swamps where the Communists would establish base areas and there was no friendly population, the free-fire zones allowed friendly troops to conduct operations freely without time-consuming requests for political clearance. They did create problems in the boundary areas around the populated centers. Sometimes in these areas, the farmers, fishermen, or wood cutters would infiltrate the free-fire zone without permission and without the knowledge of the local authorities. As a result, they were sometimes the target of attacks by fire. This obviously caused resentment regardless of the legalities involved.

In retrospect, the free-fire zone concept, for all its advantages, had some undesirable side effects. In the first place, it encouraged indiscriminate use of unobserved harassment and interdiction fire. This increased the expenditure of artillery ammunition and the actual effect on the enemy was often rather insignificant. In addition, some commanders would take the easy way out and try to control a free-fire zone by fire to the detriment of active ground operations. Thus the free-fire zone sometimes encouraged a lack of activity and aggressiveness in low level commanders.

The assignment of objectives usually depended on the nature of the objective, and the capabilities, firepower and mobility of each unit. At the beginning of the operational cooperation and coordination effort, ARVN and US units usually operated in adjacent areas. ARVN units were understandably assigned less demanding or populated areas located near axes of communication; they usually manned blocking positions for US forces. In time, ARVN forces became more combat effective and were able to conduct search and destroy operations in cooperation with US units. When cooperation was subsequently closer between the two forces, ARVN forces were able to conduct offensive operations against important objectives, in delta plains or in jungle and mountains, in conjunction with US forces or as part of the same unit. In the APACHE SNOW combined operation conducted in the A Shau Valley in May 1969, for example, the 2/3 Battalion of the ARVN 1st Infantry Division mounted a joint attack with two US airborne battalions against Hill Dong Ap Bia, a solidly entrenched enemy strong point occupied by the NVA 29th Regiment. With all-out support provided by US tactical air and artillery, ARVN and US battalions successfully liquidated the objective after two hours of fierce fighting without any unfortunate mishap or confusion.

Allocation of Resources

ARVN infantry divisions were made responsible for large tactical areas of responsibility in which the division duties were concentrated on territorial security and the support of pacification. Prior to 1969, some divisions did not have enough battalions to operate effectively. Because of territorial responsibilities, units organic to the division were scattered throughout the TAOR. When it was required to mount a large-scale offensive attack, the division was usually able to gather its forces for the effort. But this depended in a large measure on the tactical situation, enemy pressure in the TAOR, and the limited capability for replacing the divisional units by territorial forces.

To provide divisions with enough forces for operational requirements, the Joint General Staff sometimes reinforced them with units of the general reserve (the Airborne division or the Marine division) if such reinforcement was requested in the operation plan. Corps reserves were generally limited to a reaction force composed of a few ranger battalions, but even these units were not available at all times for employment. In general, units which were temporarily redeployed from static territorial missions to participate in mobile combat operations tended to be more disciplined, more audacious and more efficient at teamwork. Their combat effectiveness usually improved rapidly.

In the initial stage of US participation in the war, combat support resources for ARVN units were limited. They were usually employed to support pacification operations, defend important areas, and activities of territorial forces. When participating in combined operations with US forces, ARVN units were usually provided the following support: (1) fire support, including artillery, tactical air, and naval gunfire, (2) gunships, (3) engineers, (4) airlift (for troop movements and supplies), (5) communications, and (6) medical evacuation.

To ensure a harmonious effort among elements participating in a certain operation, the commander of a US unit providing support for ARVN units usually initiated appropriate procedures for coordination even though the supporting unit might be only a company or a battery. This was done to ensure that no relevant aspects of coordination would be overlooked. Supporting elements were designated during the planning process and liaison teams were usually attached to the ARVN units being supported. These liaison teams daily compiled the requirements of the supported unit and transmitted them to the supporting unit. Based on priorities established by the ARVN operational commander, the supporting unit reviewed support requirements and recommended the allocation of resources. Such recommendations were usually approved by the ARVN operational commander. He seldom made decisions that ran counter to recommendations made by the supporting unit commander.

When the combined operation involved the participation of several units, it was necessary to establish a Combat Support Coordination Center (CSCC). The CSCC was provided with adequate signal communications facilities and included representatives from supporting units. It was usually established at the echelon which was responsible for the conduct of the operation —corps, division, brigade or regiment —and served as a focal point for the coordination of various combat support resources. The establishment of a CSCC not only facilitated the planning of fire support; it also help speed up the exchange of information between various elements and provided an effective means for emergency personal contacts. In addition, it also helped resolve the problem of language barrier usually found in support coordination, particularly when Army Aviation units were involved.

Signal communications never constituted a seriously impeding factor in combined operations. Through the US advisory communications systems, US supporting units were able to maintain effective communications down to ARVN battalion level. With regard to US units responsible for providing direct support to ARVN forces, the best communications were those provided by the US advisory system and US liaison elements.

Logistics was usually considered as a limiting factor in combined operations. Its limitations were responsible for the short duration of combat operations conducted by ARVN units. Although the ARVN logistics system was well established at every echelon, it operated on an area basis and was not responsive enough to support ARVN units conducting protracted operations away from their rear bases. This was particularly true during the post-1968 Tet offensive period. Certain categories of supply, especially barriers and other materiels required for the construction of fire support bases, were usually not available in adequate amounts to meet operational requirements. ARVN logistics staffs were often not thoroughly conversant with the tactical situation. They were usually busy going through rigid, complicated procedures instead of providing direct and timely support for combat units. In general, they were accustomed to conducting business "as usual" and befitting a policy of normal or short duration support. Logistics was not given its necessary attention by field commanders at any echelon; it did not play its proper role in operational planning.

During the initial period of US participation, ARVN combat units had to depend almost entirely on US units for every kind of supplies including barrier and construction materiels for fire support bases, ammunition, and frequently even food. These supplies were lavishly dispensed by US units, for a certain time. Later on, particularly after the Vietnamization program was formalized, US forces provided supplies for ARVN units only on an emergency basis and if the requested items could not be provided by the Vietnamese logistics system. This was done on purpose to stimulate the development of a self-supporting ARVN logistics system and efficient logistics operation. When requesting logistics support through ARVN channels, units tended to use US advisers as leverage in the hope of obtaining adequate and timely supplies. This led in some instances to excessive and apparently wasteful demands. US advisers were usually devoted to the support of the units they advised; they were very efficient at cutting red tape and taking short cuts. In a later period, however, they confined themselves to monitoring supply requests through normal channels and interceded on behalf of ARVN units only when the request failed to get through. As a result, there was an improvement in logistics operation and increased confidence in the effectiveness of the ARVN logistics system among ARVN field units.

There was no question that ARVN units usually relied on the devoted and adequate support provided by US units which generally treated them without discrimination. This reliable support was largely instrumental in improving combat morale. Adequately supported ARVN units never faltered when participating in offensive operations against outlying enemy bases. On the contrary, they appeared to enjoy the challenge and became self-confident when authorized to participate in such operations. They certainly preferred them over the tepid pacification support activities. The employment of support assets during the initial stage of combined operations was naturally hesitant and ineffective. In time, however, ARVN units became more effective in making full use of support resources. It was obvious that, when ARVN and US units had the chance to operate together more than once, the troubles that usually plagued coordination would be ironed out and support would be more effective. In keeping with the effort to increase ARVN combat effectiveness, it was deemed necessary that additional combat support resources be provided ARVN units, particularly in Army aviation and fire support.

Use of Firepower

When large-scale operational efforts were begun in late 1966, artillery and tactical air support made available to ARVN combat units were still limited. Each ARVN infantry division at that time had only two organic 105-mm howitzer battalions, with occasional support provided by from two sections to a battery of Corps 155-mm artillery, depending on tactical requirements. In the absence of organic heavy artillery, ARVN field units usually depended on long-range fire support provided by American 8" and 175-mm artillery.

It was apparent that, given the high level of enemy activity and the sizable operational areas, such an artillery support structure was not commensurate with tactical requirements. The practice of using only organic artillery also limited the amount of firepower that could effectively be brought to bear in a certain offensive operation. Moreover, in addition to providing support for operational units, corps and divisional artillery units were also responsible for supporting Regional and Popular Forces. Artillery missions, therefore, ranged from providing direct support for regular ARVN units to attachments and direct support for Sectors (provinces) and subsectors (districts). To support territorial forces in their mission, ARVN artillery units were usually broken down into sections scattered throughout a Corps Tactical Zone in order to provide coverage for important axes of communication and populous centers.

When they were required to conduct operations well beyond bases and axes of communications, ARVN field units were usually unable to obtain adequate fire support. First, not every ARVN unit had organic artillery. Second, the ARVN artillery unit might be reluctant to deploy or be proscribed from deploying in view of its permanent territorial support mission. Third, the tactical situation might demand the heli-lift of artillery whereas ARVN artillery units during that time were not capable of this type of mobility. As a result, wherever US artillery units happened to be available for support, they usually did almost all the things normally required of a direct support unit. A US artillery unit usually provided liaison officers and forward controllers who maintained direct communications with the unit's Fire Direction Center (FDC) and could call for fires at any time. A US artillery unit could also move easily to provide the right kind of support in accordance with the maneuver plan laid out by infantry units. The usual practice employed by US forces during the period of combined operations was to assign one artillery forward controller team to each ARVN battalion and one artillery liaison officer for each ARVN major headquarters or maneuver control headquarters. The tasks performed by these liaison officers and controller teams included, apart from calling for fire missions, the planning of fire coverage for the protection of the unit and the planning of concentrated fire on objectives. The language barrier was no problem since the US adviser and his ARVN counterpart unit commander could converse in English. When assigned to an ARVN unit, the US liaison officer and the forward controller team usually relied on the US adviser and his relationship with the ARVN unit commander to transmit requirements from the Vietnamese system to US units. Since he thoroughly understood what the ARVN unit requirements were, it was just a matter of picking up the telephone or the radio handset to talk with another American at the FDC. This practice was similar to that used in Combat Support Coordination Centers. An alternative method was to put an interpreter at the American FDC to communicate with Vietnamese forward controllers or batteries. Over a period of time, the use of an interpreter was not necessary because Vietnamese forward controllers, who were usually young officers, could use English to control fire through the radio system.

The shortage of artillery assets required for the simultaneous support of different missions generated the need for tactical air to provide support for operational units. Since tactical air invariably achieved excellent results, ARVN unit commanders and certain US advisers developed the tendency to rely entirely on tactical air for support even when both tactical air and artillery were available and both were equally effective for their purpose. During that period of time, the Vietnamese Air Force was capable of providing only a little over ten sorties per day for each Corps Tactical Zone. Operational units, as a result, depended mostly on the powerful firepower of US tactical air when there was a requirement to level solid enemy fortifications or bases, especially if these objectives were located in jungle or mountainous areas. ARVN operational units also depended on US gunships for immediate support after initial contact was made with the enemy. In general, coordination and control of tactical air support was smoothly operated through the US advisory communications system.

The powerful US tactical air and artillery firepower provided ARVN combat units with a most effective and accurate support, and assisted them in winning several major battles. Vietnamese commanders and troops alike were entirely confident of this support effectiveness. This confidence, in turn, enhanced their morale and remarkably improved unit combat effectiveness. The lavish use of firepower, however, became ingrained in Vietnamese tactics and became a bad habit. Whenever contact was made with the enemy, regardless of size or firepower, ARVN units invariably requested all-out fire support by artillery and tactical air; they took less interest in the unit organic weapons, light or heavy. This over-reliance on heavy firepower more often than not amounted to sheer waste and overkill, and resulted in much human loss and property damage to the local population living in the area of operation.

To minimize human loss and property damage to the population, MACV and the Joint General Staff jointly published operational procedures regulating the use of firepower which were binding on both US and ARVN units when they conducted operations in populated areas. These procedures have been presented earlier in this chapter. Given the nature of the Vietnam war, however, it was usually difficult, if not impossible, for operational units to accurately estimate the size and potential of enemy forces before contact was made and before the objective had been liquidated. There were times when a whole hamlet was leveled and only a dozen or so enemy troops were destroyed with it. In contrast, there were also times when friendly units incurred heavy losses because of inadequate fire support. Save for a few cases of negligence, no unit commander ever wanted to cause losses or injuries to his innocent countrymen. His natural inclination as troop commander, however, was to minimize losses to his men even when this was apt to cause damage and casualties to the populace. Only the most experienced field commanders could effectively employ firepower with accuracy and tailor it to the size and nature of the objective.

In addition to tactical support artillery, naval and tactical and strategic air firepower were also employed in unusual, and unobservable fire missions to attack and destroy enemy bases and those areas where an enemy troop concentration or movement was reported. There was also the nightly interdiction and harassment artillery fire. These types of fire were effective when they were carefully planned. Artillery interdiction and harassment fire, however, was not carefully planned. It was usually applied in a haphazard and unruly manner, particularly in the Mekong Delta, chiefly for the purpose of enhancing the morale of RF and PF troops in isolated outposts.

Civilian Evacuation, Casualties and Property Damage

After 1959 when the war entered a more active phase in South Vietnam, many innocent civilians, caught in crossfire between opposing sides, were killed or wounded. Most of these casualties occurred among the rural population. The civilian casualty rate increased proportionately with the fighting level and reached an all-time high in early 1968 when the Communists launched the Tet offensive against cities and major population centers throughout the country.

Civilian casualties had many causes but most frequently were due to enemy booby traps or to mortar and rocket fires. Civilians also died from stray fire during battles, or from friendly aerial bombings and occasionally from the deliberate use of terror by Communist forces. The most worrisome problém in this regard was the deliberate Communist tactic of precipitating a battle in a populated area. If the friendly forces declined to fight in order to avoid casualties and damage to the friendly population, the Communist would strengthen their control of the area. On the other hand, if a battle ensued by choice or was unavoidable, the civilian population suffered casualties and damage. This not only caused resentment against both the GVN and the Communists but required an expensive and time-consuming rebuilding process to restore the physical damage and for the people to regain their morale and confidence.

Civilian casualties and their causes are presented in Table 1 for the period from 1967 to 1970. It should be noted, however, that casualty figures in Vietnam were notoriously unreliable and that it was most difficult to determine whether the casualties were caused by Communists or friendly action, or both.

Table 1 — Civilian Casualties and Causes[2]

Mines, mortar and booby-traps[3]	Small-arms fire	Shelling and bombing	Total
1967 15,253	9,785	18,811	43,849
1968 31,244	15,107	28,052	74,403
1969 24,648	11,814	16,183	52,645
1970 22,049	7,650	8,607	38,306

[2]"Annex K", Statement of Ambassador William E. Colby, Deputy to COMUSMACV for CORDS, before the Subcommittee on Refugees and Escapees of the Senate Committee on the Judiciary, 21 April 1971.

[3]The enemy sometimes used unexploded bombs and artillery shells as booby-traps.

As of late 1968, however, civilian casualties were gradually reduced as a result of improved security which was achieved throughout most of the countryside by the pacification effort. Regulations for the use of firepower were constantly updated by MACV and the JGS and their strict application was enforced by both US and ARVN forces when conducting operations in populated areas. Operational techniques such as the soft cordon,[4] for example, which was characterized by a maximum limitation of firepower with a view to minimizing casualties and property damages to the civilian population, were especially encouraged. So were plans to neutralize the enemy "mini-bases" which were thoroughly rigged with mines and booby-traps, especially in IV Corps Tactical Zone. It was also recommended that artillery harassment and interdiction fire be cut to a minimum. Violations of fire employment regulations which caused casualities to the local population were carefully studied to determine those responsible and also served as a basis for equitable compensation and relief to the victims.

When accidents, casualities and property damage were caused to the civilian population by US units, immediate steps were taken to comfort and assist the victims of these units. Injured people were given first aid and immediately evacuated to the nearest US or RVN medical facility. This medical assistance and care was continued until the victims completely recovered. Also transportation was arranged for relatives to make visits. Damaged properties or houses were immediately repaired, rebuilt or equitably compensated.

---

[4]The soft cordon is characterized by limited use of firepower resulting in minimum property damages and injury to civilians, and slow, painstaking searches of villages and suspicious areas by the sweeping and cordon forces. The cordon force serves a dual purpose: it blocks, and at the same time, searches. The so-called blocking positions are not static defensive positions but are moving, searching troops who make detailed searches. They occupy and serve as a "noose" around the cordoned area. The protracted occupation of an area causes the concealed enemy to become impatient and hungry, forcing them to reveal their hiding places. See also Lam Son 260/NEVADA EAGLE operation later in the chapter.

Skirmishes between the two sides constituted a major source of danger for the civilians and their families who resided in the area. To them, friendly aerial bombings and strafings were as deadly as the enemy rockets, mortar shells, mines and booby-traps. The big difference was that US units always looked after the victims with care and swiftness, regardless of who caused the injuries. This instilled comfort and confidence among the population. By nature, the Vietnamese peasant is resilient and accustomed to hardship. As a matter of fact, he never expected to receive so much help from US units if anything happened to him, his family or his property. This help was a necessary effort which was both humanitarian and psychologically advantageous insofar as the Vietnamese people were concerned. If all civilian casualties and property damages could have been compensated or repaired as swiftly and as fairly, it would have been a great source of comfort for the unfortunate civilian living in the midst of a war.

The evacuation of the civilian population during combat operations usually created many difficult problems chiefly when it was necessary to displace and resettle a large number of people. During Operation Cedar Falls conducted by II FFV in December 1966, about 6,000 civilians living in the Ben Suc area were evacuated to Phu Cuong district in Binh Duong province. The Hickory/Lam Son 54 combined operation jointly conducted by the US 3d Marine Division and the ARVN 1st Infantry Division in May 1967 displaced a total of 13,000 people form the DMZ area to Cam Lo district in Quang Tri province. Those were but a few examples of large-scale civilian evacuation occasioned by friendly operations.

The most frustrating thing about civilian evacuations was that they could never be extensively planned in advance. This was due primarily to the necessity of keeping operational plans secret. Coordination with the local government and other GVN or US agencies for the evacuation of the local population was allowed only after the operation had been in progress. In the few instances in which advance coordination was necessary, it was limited to a few high-ranking officials. As a result, deficiencies were bound to occur during the initial stage of the evacuation.

Civilian evacuation was a responsibility of ARVN units and the local government. In the performance of this task, they were supported by US units and civilian agencies which provided abundant transportation and supplies. The displacement of the populace and their belongings, therefore, was usually smooth and rapid, regardless of size and load. Despite the lack of advance planning, Vietnamese officials who were experienced and familiar with this task could always run the operation without difficulty.

Resettlement of the displaced population remained, however, a thorny problem in the evacuation process. This subject cannot be discussed at length within the scope of this monograph since it was a rather complex socio-political problem. In general, very few Vietnamese, and the peasants in particular, were willing to relinquish their land, their houses, and their normal habitat for a safe, new life elsewhere even though threatened by the constant dangers of war. After they had been displaced and resettled in some local refugee center, most of these reluctant refugees found it hard to make a living as soon as relief was removed. Consequently, some were forced to live on relatives and some would try to return to their old place if that was still possible. Thus, with the exception of large scale and permanent resettlement projects, very few of those makeshift resettlement centers that mushroomed overnight in the wake of military operations could effectively serve their purpose for any long period of time.

Special Planning Considerations

Operations conducted in desolate and remote jungle or mountainous areas necessitated the employment of tactics which differed greatly from those employed in operations conducted in the flatter and more open, populated areas. This was tantamount to prosecuting two different kinds of war. In both types of operations, cooperation and coordination between participating US and ARVN forces were deemed necessary and mutually beneficial.

In the case of operations conducted in remote jungle or mountainous areas, however, the planning and coordination process was much less complicated since it did not involve many of the problems and constraints found in populated areas. Such operations were usually conducted in areas which harbored enemy logistics bases, troop cantonment havens or major headquarters, political or military. These areas generally were sheltering North Vietnamese main force units. Planning for these operations was exactly like planning for conventional battles. The usual tactic was to employ B-52, tactical air, artillery and naval firepower on the objective, followed by a swift troop movement into the objective area to exploit results. Both US and ARVN training, organization, and equipment were properly geared for such operations, operations in which firepower and mobility were most valuable advantages. To make rapid and accurate use of tactical air and gunships and also to avoid identification errors between the two participating forces in this type terrain, much care and attention was given to the assignment of boundaries and objectives during the planning process.

The allocation of combat support and logistics resources for ARVN units during the entire operation was deemed necessary to maintain their sustained combat effectiveness on a par with US units. When provided with adequate support and when all requirements were fulfilled, ARVN units could make substantial contributions to these operations. Familiarity with the terrain and the enemy, and adaptability to the environment were their natural advantages. Their endurance and resiliency also helped them cross jungles and mountains without much difficulty. They were particularly efficient in conducting reconnaissance with long range reconnaissance patrols, particularly when these patrols were jointly organized. In general, when planning for operations in remote or jungle areas, the maximum exploitation of combat capabilities of each of the participating units, and the effective use of combat support assets were considered the key to success.

In contrast, when US units or ARVN regular units operated in populated areas or participated in the pacification program, they were faced with many complex problems. Not only did they have to fight the enemy, they had to also provide protection for villages and hamlets. And the most difficult part of it all was the goal of doing all these things without causing damage and casualties, or even antagonizing the local population. Civil action efforts played a very important role in such operations. The most practical civil action effort was to limit the use of firepower, but this firepower constituted the great advantage of the US units. American reactions to enemy provocations, regarded by the Americans as defensive acts, were regarded by the population as offensive acts since it was American bombs and shells which caused the casualties and damages. Fire limitations therefore were a central problem. The difficulty lay not in persuading troops to limit the use of firepower, but in the decisions made in the heat of battle concerning the use of artillery, gunships, and tactical air. The natural inclination of unit commanders of all echelons was to minimize losses to their own men rather than losses to the civilian population. However, in a war in which political considerations usually outweighed military requirements, a certain compromise had to be made in order to win over the people's hearts and minds. In addition to the limited and controlled use of firepower, curfew time and free-fire zones also needed to be made flexible, and tailored to seasonal changes in each locality so as not to obstruct the normal life cycle of the local population.

Before being introduced into an area of operation, units should be thoroughly oriented on local customs and manners in order to avoid awkward situations which would interfere with the development of good rapport with the population. Only in such a way could there be a genuine cooperation on the part of the local population. Particular attention should also be given to preventing the enemy from taking propaganda advantage of our mistakes.

In addition to difficulties that arose from relations with the friendly population, operational units had other problems such as the local government, military authorities, and territorial forces in the area of operation. Coordination with them was necessary in order to combine effectively the military and civilian efforts. The planning for operations in populated areas thus required detailed and careful preparation and close coordination and cooperation among all the elements involved. US units usually combined daily tactical efforts with a powerful dose of psywar and civil action in an attempt to achieve good rapport with the local population. In general, operations of this type required flexibility, not only in force organization but also in tactics, techniques, and the utilization of support assets.

US units certainly had to face many complex problems in addition to their inherent disadvantages in language, culture and race. Despite all this, they succeeded admirably in many instances in bringing about a well founded confidence and security for the population, even in areas where the population had lived for a long time under Communist influence.

Operation DELAWARE/LAM SON 216

Operation Delaware/Lam Son 216 in the A Shau valley was a typical case of combined operations conducted in remote and jungle or mountainous areas with the purpose of destroying enemy logistics bases and command headquarters. It was planned in the wake of the enemy 1968 Tet offensive as one in a series of major combined efforts striking into enemy bases which heretofore were considered as inviolable.

US and ARVN forces were then taking the initiative. Driven back from cities and population centers, NVA units retreated toward jungle or mountainous redoubts to replace losses, refit, and prepare themselves for the next wave of attacks. Launching major offensive operations against enemy bases was a great challenge for ARVN units at that time as their principal effort during the previous few years had been concentrated on pacification support. Most combat actions by ARVN units had been confined to securing or to search-and-destroy operations of very short duration, usually conducted in some nearby foothill areas.

ARVN units had incurred sizable losses during the intense fighting that characterized the initial phase of the enemy general offensive. There were serious losses of experienced cadre and troops. Some ARVN battalions had been reduced to a strength of approximately 100 men, and replacements were all new recruits. This made ARVN combat effectiveness somewhat questionable in the eyes of US commanders, in particular those who were already dubious as to their effectiveness. Indeed, in the beginning, most US units were unenthusiastic about the proposed combined operations. This was understandable enough, since cooperation with ARVN units might turn out to be an additional burden to the US units.

The Delaware/Lam Son 216 combined operation took place in the A Shau valley, in the western part of I CTZ, in mid-April 1968. This was the first major effort to penetrate this longtime enemy held area since 1966 when a US Special Forces camp there was overrun. The A Shau valley, which included the A Luoi airfield, was surrounded by extremely rugged mountainous areas covered with dense jungle. Located near the Laotian border, it was crisscrossed by a road-system which linked the enemy bases and sanctuaries in Laotian territory with his advance bases located in the foothill area west of I CTZ coastal plain. *(See Map 4)* The weather in the A Shau valley areas was unpredictable; it was usually cloudy during the monsoon season. The objective area was confirmed as one of the NVA major logistics bases. Intelligence reports estimated enemy forces in the area to include: a command and control headquarters, one engineer regiment, one transportation battalion, one signal battalion, one anti-aircraft battalion, armor elements, and base protection units.

The concept of maneuver set forth in the operational plan stated that the US 1st Air Cavalry Division in coordination with the ARVN 1st Infantry Division was to conduct a heliborne operation into the A Shau valley, occupy the A Luoi airfield, and organize reconnaissance patrols in force. On D-day, the 3d Brigade, 1st ACD, with 3 battalions and support artillery elements, was to land north of the A Luoi airfield, establish fire support bases, destroy by fire enemy positions around the airfield, and conduct reconnaissance in force in the area. On D+1, the 3d Brigade was to continue operations while the radio relay terminal at A Shau began to function. On D+2, the 1st Brigade, 1st ACD, with 3 battalions and support artillery elements, was to land and occupy the A Luoi airfield, and conduct reconnaissance in force in the area. On D+2, engineer and signal equipment and an initial logistics element were to be helilifted into the A Luoi airfield to begin repair to the airfield.

Then, on D+4, the 3d Regiment, 1st ARVN Infantry Division, was to land into the area south of the A Luoi airfield with support artillery elements and to conduct reconnaissance in force. On D+5, the airfield would begin operation with C-7A aircraft, and on D+6, with C-123 aircraft. Reconnaissance in force operations were to be conducted throughout the A Shau valley until termination of the combined operations. The fire support plan gave priority to the 3d Brigade on D-Day. All landings were to be supported by artillery and tactical air. Air coverage was to

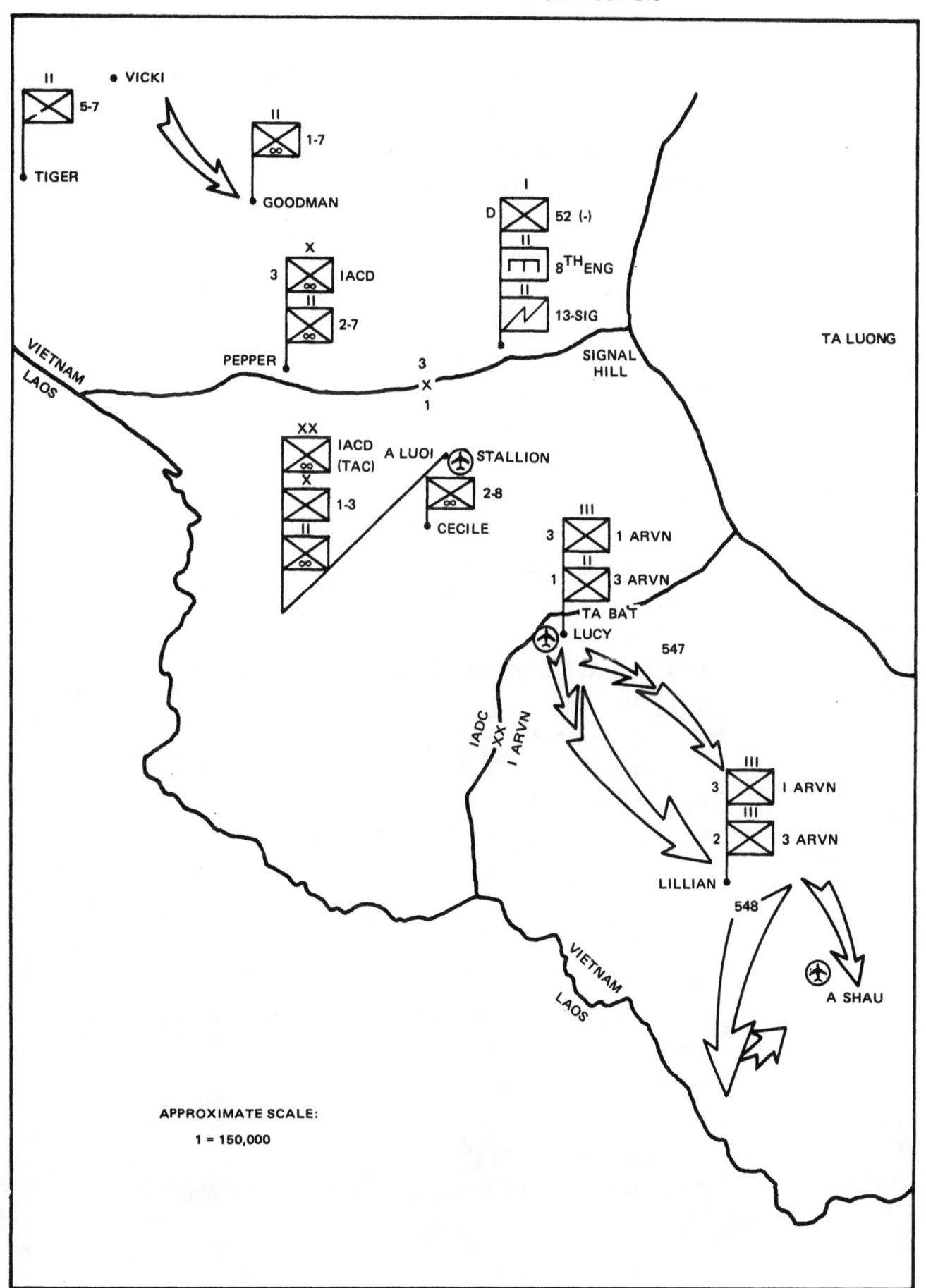

MAP 4. — OPERATION DELAWARE/LAM-SON 216

to be provided by fixed-wing aircraft and gunships during landings.

On the US side, maneuver forces included:

    1st Brigade, 1st Air Cavalry Division:

        1-8 Cav., 2-8 Cav., 1-12 Cav.

        2-19 Arty (DS), A Battery, 1-30 Arty (GSR)

        A Co, 8th Engr. (GSR)

        2 Sqds, 25th Inf.

        Det. 11th Pathfinder Plat.

        Fwd Spt. Tm., 13th Sig. (DS)

        Tm., 191st MI Co.

        Tm., 5th Weather Sqdn.

        Plat., 545th MP Co.

        Tm., 246th Psyop. Co.

        Det., Co. D 52 Inf.

        FSE, Div. Spt Cmd. (DS).

    3d Brigade, 1st Air Cavalry Division:

        1-7 Cav., 2-7 Cav., 5-7 Cav.

        1-21 Arty (DS), C Battery, 1-30 Arty (GSR)

        C Co, 8th Engr. (DS)

        2 sqds, 34th Inf.

        Det, 11th Pathfinder Plat.

        Fwd. Spt Tm, 13th Sig.

        Tm., 191st MI Co.

        Tm., 5th Weather Sqdn.

        Plat., 545th MP Co.

        Tm., 245th Psyop. Co.

        FSE, Div. Spt Cmd (DS)

    On the Vietnamese side, maneuver forces included:

        3d Regiment, 1st Infantry Division

        1st Battalion, 3d Regt.

        2d Battalion, 3d Regt.

        2d Battalion, 1st Regt.

        C Battery, 1-12 Arty. (DS)

US support to Vietnamese forces included:
- A Battery, 6-33 Arty, US (GSR)
- Arty LNO and FO tms., 1st ACD Div. Arty.
- AT Sect (106 RR), D 1-9 Cav.
- Plat., C Co, 14th Engr. (DS)
- Fwd. Spt. Tm. (VHF), 13th Sig. Bn.

On 19 April (D-day), the 3d Brigade, 1st Air Cavalry Division made initial heliborne landings in the A Shau valley. The 5-7 Cav., supported by the 11th Aviation Group, landed and established Landing Zone Tiger, while the 1-7 Cav. landed on LZ Vicki. The direct support artillery battery intended for the 5-7 Cav was also moved to LZ Tiger. Despite extensive preparatory fire and the protection of landing approaches provided by elements of the 1-9 Cav., enemy anti-aircraft was still very active. A total of 23 helicopters were hit, of which 10 were destroyed. Both the 5-7 and 1-7 Cav. met no enemy resistance during landings, but the helilift of the 1-7 Cav. was delayed due to intense enemy anti-aircraft fire and bad weather. Also, because site preparation required extensive engineer work, the movement of a direct support artillery battery into LZ Vicki was not completed as planned.

In conjunction with landings of the 3d Brigade, Company E of the 52d Infantry (-), two engineer squads of the 8th Engineer Battalion, and elements of the 13th Signal Battalion were helilifted to a high mountain peak to install a radio relay site at Signal Hill.

On 20 and 21 April, the heliborne movement of troops into the area north of A Shau valley was continued; Company B (+) of the 2-7 Cav. landed and established LZ Pepper. But other troop and supply movements were delayed because of bad weather and extremely heavy rains. The 1-7 Cav. also began maneuvering from LZ Vicki to seize and secure LZ Goodman, while forces on Signal Hill continued work on a landing zone and relay site preparation. An enemy probing attack on Signal Hill caused 4 killed and 3 wounded.

Then the 5-7 Cav. initiated activities in the vicinity of LZ Tiger, concentrating on the interdiction of Route 548 which ran into the A Shau valley from Laos. Searches were conducted in force in order to find and neutralize enemy anti-aircraft positions. The weather, meanwhile, continued to impede all air activities during the day of 21 April. But the 1-7 Cav. continued to overcome the rugged terrain and succeeded in occupying LZ Goodman. On its way to this LZ, the 1-7 Cav. found and destroyed 2 Russian-made bulldozers. The 5-7 Cav., meanwhile, continued its search operations around LZ Tiger, and work also progressed on Signal Hill, where a small D-4 bulldozer was brought in to clear the landing zone. In the early afternoon of 21 April, a section (two 105-mm howitzers) of A Battery, 1-21 Artillery Battalion was helilifted into a firing position on Signal Hill, from where it provided all night support for B Company of the 2-7 at LZ Pepper.

On 22 and 23 April, with improved weather, the 3d Brigade was able to complete its troop movements into A Shau. The 2-7 Cav. and the Brigade headquarters landed at LZ Pepper, and by early afternoon of 22 April, the 1-7 Cav. had completed its defense positions at LZ Goodman. The 5-7 Cav., meanwhile, continued its search operations, concentrating its effort on the areas west and south of LZ Tiger. Benefiting from good weather the movement of artillery units was completed during the day of 23 April. A direct support 105-mm battery landed at LZ Goodman, and another at LZ Pepper. An additional 155-mm howitzer battery was also helilifted into LZ Goodman by early morning the following day.

On 24 and 25 April, after having completed its troop movements into A Shau, the 3d Brigade continued reconnaissance in force operations, by spreading out from LZs Tiger, Goodman and Pepper in an extensive search effort. The 1-7 Cav. found and captured three flat-bed trucks and three 37-mm anti-aircraft guns. On 24 April, the 1st Brigade helilifted its 2-8 Cav. into LZ Cecile together with a direct support battery (-) of three 105-mm howitzers, but the movement was later suspended because of bad weather. On 25 April, the weather improved again, and the 1st Brigade quickly moved its remaining battalions and the 1-8 Cav. into the same LZ. As soon as it landed, the 2-8 initiated reconnaissance in force activities south and west of LZ Cecile while the 1-8 Cav. assumed the defense of LZ Stallion and pushed its companies north in a search effort. The 1-12 Cav., meanwhile, operated south and east of the LZ.

From 26 to 28 April, the movement of artillery units into LZ Stallion for the support of the 1st Brigade was continued, and reconnaissance in force activities were intensified throughout both the 1st and 3d Brigade areas of operation. Friendly forces also began to make light to medium sporadic contacts with the enemy. During their extensive searches, they found and captured several enemy 37-mm anti-aircraft guns which were mostly scattered throughout the area north of A Shau valley, and many important caches of all kinds of supplies, particularly in the area called the "punchbowl" which was located in the 1st Brigade AO. Tactical air and artillery provided powerful support for units conducting the search effort. Also, as of 26 April, heavy drops of materiel and equipment by C-130 cargo planes were delivered at the southern end of A Luoi airfield.

From 29 April to 3 May, the ARVN 1-3 Battalion and the command post of the 3d Regiment were air lifted into the area of operation, south of the A Shau Valley where they established LZ Lucy. They were followed by the 2-3 Battalion on 30 April and the 2-1 Battalion and the regimental direct support 105-mm battery on 1 May. This completed the deployment of the 3d ARVN Regiment. Like the US 1st and 3d Brigades, all three ARVN battalions conducted reconnaissance in force operations as soon as their landings were completed. Their companies spread out around LZ Lucy in search of the enemy.

During this time, US units continued their reconnaissance in force effort with encouraging results. Most remarkable was the skillful maneuvering of the 2-8 Cav. into the "Punchbowl" base area which was heavily protected by enemy forces. Artillery and tactical air firepower was used extensively in this maneuver and destroyed several solidly fortified enemy positions in this area. By 3 May, the 2-8 Cav. was in full control of this area. Tons of enemy supplies were captured and 30 NVA troops were killed.

In conjunction with these operations, the introduction of additional support elements into LZ Stallion was continued. The 8th Engineer Battalion worked day and night on the A Luoi airfield and by 1 May, the airfield began operation with the landing of C-7As and C-123s. By

3 May, work on the lengthening of the airstrip was completed and the airfield began to accommodate C-130s as well. In the meantime, the 1st Air Cavalry Division Tactical CP, supported by elements of the 13th Signal Battalion, began to operate as of 1800 hours of 28 April.

From 4 to 7 May, after search operations in the vicinity of LZ Lucy had been completed, the ARVN 3d Regiment began conducting offensive attacks in a southeasterly direction along both banks of the Rao Lao River with its 2-1 Battalion to the north and the 2-3 Battalion to the south. The 1-3 Battalion, meanwhile, stayed back for the defense of LZ Lucy, which was now reinforced by A Battery of the 6-33 Artillery Battalion. The 3d Regiment progress met only scattered enemy resistance although ARVN troops found many important supply caches. By 7 May, units of the 3d Regiment had advanced to the limit of maximum 105-mm range from LZ Lucy. On 7 May, the 1-12 Cav. replaced the 1-3 Battalion for the defense of LZ Lucy. Another direct support artillery battery was helilifted from LZ Stallion to LZ Lucy. The 2-8 Cav., meanwhile, continued searching the "Punch Bowl" base area, retrieving enemy-captured weapons, and destroying enemy supply caches. The 1-8 also continued securing LZ Stallion by deploying rear company and platoon-size search parties to the south and east of the LZ.

While keeping up its search operations, the 3d Brigade found several supply caches and electrical and telephone wires crisscrossing the valley. Its fire support bases, which straddled the access routes to the valley, were constantly harassed by enemy B-40, 82-mm mortar, and 122-mm rocket fire.

On 8 and 9 May, the ARVN 3d Regiment moved two additional artillery batteries by helilift into LZ Lillian to extend the fire support range toward the south. LZ Lillian had been secured by the 2-3 Battalion the day before. With this additional artillery support, the 3d Regiment resumed its offensive attacks toward the A Shau airfield and soon covered the entire valley with its search parties. The US 1st and 3d Brigades, meanwhile, continued operations in their areas of responsibility. In addition to reconnaissance in force operations, the 3d Regiment and 3d Brigade also initiated extensive preparation of obstacles to impede enemy activities after the extraction of friendly forces. The direct support engineer company of the 3d Brigade established, within the brigade AO, 32 separate obstacles which completely blocked Route 542 south of LZ Tiger. The engineer platoon supporting the 3d Regiment established 16 obstacles within the regiment's AO.

From 10 to 16 May, after completing reconnaissance-in-force operations and establishing obstacles, the 3d Brigade and 3d Regiment began to withdraw on 10 May. The 5-7 Cav. and 1-7 Cav. and artillery units moved out of LZs Tiger and Goodman by helicopters on 10 May. At the same time, the 2-1 Battalion of the 3d Regiment was helilifted to LZ Stallion (A Luoi airfield) where it boarded fixed-wing aircraft and was moved to Quang Tri. From LZ Pepper, the 2-7Cav. (-), the 3d Brigade headquarters and the artillery battery were extracted to Camp Evans. The extraction of the 3d Brigade was completed on 11 May. The 3d Regiment also completed its extraction by helicopter, to include the 1-3 and 2-3 Battalions, the regimental headquarters and the artillery battery.

Also, during the period from 10 to 15 May, the 1st Brigade continued its activities and established obstacles in its area of operation. In the meantime, logistical elements were helilifted from LZ Stallion to Camp Evans while heavy equipment were moved out by fixed-wing aircraft. Heavy rains that began in the afternoon of 11 May, however, rendered the A Luoi airfield completely unusable after that day. After establishing a total of 26 obstacles, the 1st Brigade continued to provide security for LZ Stallion during the time logistics and support elements were extricated. On 12 May, the tactical CP of the 1st Air Cavalry Division and elements of the 13th Signal Battalion were helilifted to Camp Evans. On 15 May, the 1st Brigade began extricating its units, the 1-8 Cav., 1-12 Cav., the Brigade headquarters and artillery elements from LZs Lucy and Stallion. The last units to move out of A Shau valley were the 2-8 Cav. and its artillery battery, which were helilifted out of LZ Cecile on 16 May, and the remaining elements of the 13th Signal Battalion at Signal Hill which were moved to Camp Evans on the same day.

Operation Delaware/Lam Son 216 was terminated at 1100 hours on 17 May 1968 after all US and ARVN participating units had been redeployed to designated areas and were ready for new assignments. The results achieved by the operation were substantial. Enemy casualties amounted to 425 killed, 3 captured, and 7 returnees. Weapons, ammunition, and materiels captured included: 2 bulldozers, 73 wheeled vehicles, 3 tracked vehicles, 1 tank, 13 anti-aircraft weapons, 2,371 individual weapons, 31 crew-served weapons, 42,347 large caliber rounds, 1,521 mines and grenades, 168,879 small arm and 12.7-mm rounds and 71,805 lbs of food stores.

Continuing its combat activities, the 3d ARVN Regiment, once again in close coordination and cooperation with the 3d Air Cavalry Brigade, initiated another major combined operation just one day after the completion of operation Delaware/Lam Son 216. This operation was launched on 18 May against Secret Base 114, an important enemy base located deep in the jungles of western Thua Thien. The attached 2-1 Battalion was first deployed into the enemy base area where it established FSB Miguel. On the same day, before dark, the regimental headquarters and one 105-mm direct support artillery battery were helilifted into the LZ. The following day, 19 May, two other battalions of the 3d ARVN Regiment completed their deployment into the area of operation. The 1-3 Battalion landed and secured LZ Jose, east of Base 114. The 2-3 Battalion was also moved to LZ Jose.

As soon as the troop landings were completed, these two battalions conducted offensive operations southwestward, searching out enemy main force units and striking into the enemy tactical headquarters and logistics installations. During the entire period of operation, units of the 3d ARVN Regiment engaged the enemy in medium to heavy firefights throughout the area of operation. They discovered and destroyed many important control headquarters and logistics installations of the enemy. What was most remarkable about this follow-on operation was its duration. In close cooperation and coordination with the US 3d Air Cavalry Brigade, the 3d Regiment conducted sweeping operations and fought for 116 consecutive days.

Some Communist trucks and weapons captured in the A Shau valley, ICTZ, Operation DELAWARE/LAM SON 216, April 1968.

Farther to the north, similar combined operations were conducted by the ARVN 1st Regiment and the US 1st Air Cavalry Brigade. In close coordination with each other, both units launched repeated attacks against enemy Base 101, west of Quang Tri province. These operations were also sustained for a long time and brought about encouraging results.

DELAWARE/LAM SON 216 was the first large scale combined operation conducted by forces of the US 1st Air Cavalry Division and the ARVN 1st Infantry Division against an enemy base located deep in the jungle and mountains. Its success required a close and constant coordination and a mutual trust between the participating forces. Since it was a difficult and hazardous mission, the US 1st Air Cavalry Division at first was not enthusiastic about cooperating with ARVN forces. The combat effectiveness of the ARVN 3d Regiment was held in serious doubt by US forces. What they were unaware of was the high morale and discipline of this unit. Troops and commanders of the 3d Regiment were particularly proud when they were given the chance to operate alongside the 1st Air Cavalry Division, a unit whose combat prowess and firepower they held in high regard.

It was understandable that during this operation, the ARVN 3d Regiment was assigned the least difficult objective. The results obtained by this ARVN unit, therefore, were only modest, but the psychological impact of its participation in a difficult operation was extremely favorable among other ARVN units and the population. The operational plan was well executed and the performance of all units was excellent. This was chiefly due to a high degree of cooperation and coordination between US and ARVN forces.

The operation was also a successful test that brought about mutual trust and gave a good impetus to combined activities of US and ARVN forces in the 11th DTZ (Quang Tri and Thua Thien provinces). As a result, coordination and cooperation became exceptionally good at the sector and subsector levels between ARVN and US forces on one side and territorial forces on the other. Difficulties and troubles, if any, occurred only when US and ARVN combined their efforts for the first time. After the initial steps had been taken, a spirit of cooperation and teamwork rapidly developed and in time led to continued success. Some reluctance to cooperate existed at first on the part of a few American commanders because they were uneasy about ARVN combat effectiveness. However, after they had seen ARVN units prove themselves in combat, their prejudice disappeared and they realized that cooperation with ARVN combat elements could help make their task easier and contribute to success.

A great benefit of combined operations of this type was the rapid improvement of ARVN combat effectiveness. The 3d Regiment, until operation DELAWARE/LAMSON 216, was generally considered mediocre among ARVN regiments. But after a few months operating alongside the US 3d Air Cavalry Brigade in enemy base area 114, the 3d Regiment achieved marked progress and became one of the best ARVN combat units.

Operation LAM SON 260/NEVADA EAGLE

Operation LAM SON 260/NEVADA EAGLE was an ARVN-US combined operation conducted in the Vinh Loc district of Thua Thien province in mid-September 1968. The objective of the operation was to destroy enemy local units, eliminate his infrastructure and guerrillas, and ultimately restore local government control and security for the local population.

Vinh Loc district was a long and narrow island sandwiched between the sea and Thuy Tu Sound and located some 20 miles east-southeast of Hue city. Its length was 25 miles and its width, about 3 miles. Before the enemy 1968 Tet offensive, Vinh Loc had been a prosperous and relatively secure district. Its population of approximately 50,000 lived mostly by fishing and farming. During the Tet offensive, the enemy took advantage of the deteriorating situation and infiltrated local troops into the area to reinforce and expand his infrastructure. Several villages and hamlets came under enemy control. The enemy's ultimate goal was to turn Vinh Loc district into an impenetrable safe haven and staging area for his local units. As of that time, local government control was effective only in the eastern portion of the island where about 29,000 local inhabitants and 12,500 refugees lived. The remaining 8,500 of the district population were virtually under enemy control. Enemy local forces in the area were estimated at anywhere from 2 companies to 2 battalions, not including the guerrillas and infrastructure.

From March to August 1968, Vietnamese territorial forces and US units separately conducted several screening operations in the enemy-infested area without any significant results. In general, when operating by themselves, RF and PF units met with forceful reactions from enemy local units and never fulfilled their mission. On their part, US units usually swept through objectives in the area of operation for only a short time, then quickly moved out. As a result, enemy forces either put up token resistance or avoided contact altogether by hiding themselves and waiting out operating forces. This enemy tactic was well known by the local government and Vietnamese and American units. Nothing could be effectively done against it, however, because separate efforts never gathered enough forces for a saturation effort and the idea of cooperation and coordination was yet to be willingly shared by the commanders concerned.

It was decided then that only a combined effort of US, ARVN, RF and the local government could achieve the desired results. Operation LAM SON 260/NEVADA EAGLE was the product of detailed planning and close coordination between operating forces of both sides. The overall operational concept was to achieve tactical surprise by quick action. Strict security measures were therefore enforced to avoid disclosure of the operation plan. The last coordinating session to finalize the plan, for example, was held off until the day before D-day which was scheduled to be on 11 September. As a result, operational orders were issued to participating forces only at the last minute, allowing them just enough time to prepare for action. In addition, reconnaissance over the target area was held at a minimum; also, operational headquarters and support units were to move into position only after H-hour.

The operational plan first called for a cordon to be surreptiously put in place utilizing all resources available. The key to success rested on denying the enemy any advance warning signs of the operation.

Then quick action was to follow with the landings of heliborne forces on the beaches. After landings, operating forces would sweep across the island during the first day. The move was designed to fragment enemy forces into separate elements and interdict all communication between them. Care was also taken to block all the routes that the enemy usually employed to evade friendly troops.

To minimize damages and casualties to the local population, preparatory fire was to be held to a minimum and support fire was to be employed only in case of significant resistance. Special precautions were taken to avoid unnecessary destruction. For the effective control and screening of the population, each operating unit was accompanied by representatives of the local government. All youths of draft age were to be temporarily detained, including those who possessed legal identification papers.

Then a careful and minute search would be conducted throughout the island. As soon as they were introduced into their areas of operations, participating units would quickly fan out and search. The search was to be thorough and systematic. Information provided by the local government, population, prisoners, or returnees and any other sources would be instantly exploited to give focus to the search effort.

The operational plan carefully detailed the task organization of participating forces which were composed of blocking forces, a maneuver element, and control and special elements. *(Chart 7)*

1. Blocking forces consisted of 2 battalions of the 54th Regiment, 1st ARVN Infantry Division, deployed in Phu Thu district; 1 company of the 1/501st, 101st US Airborne Division, deployed on the Phu Vang — Vinh Loc border for 10 September only; 7 PF platoons, 5 of which were deployed to Vinh Loc and 2 to Phu Vang; 2 ARVN Coastal Groups (12th and 13th), 1 Patrol Boat River Group, USN, and 1 Patrol Air Cushion Vehicle Group, USN, all deployed on the Thuy Tu Sound; and 1 Swift Boat Group, USN, in the ocean screening the coast.

2. The maneuver element was composed of the 1st Battalion, 54th Regiment, 1st ARVN Infantry Division, assigned to the western half of the island; the 1/501 Battalion, 2d Brigade, 101st Airborne Division, assigned to the eastern half; 1 squadron of the 7th Armored Cavalry Regiment, 1st

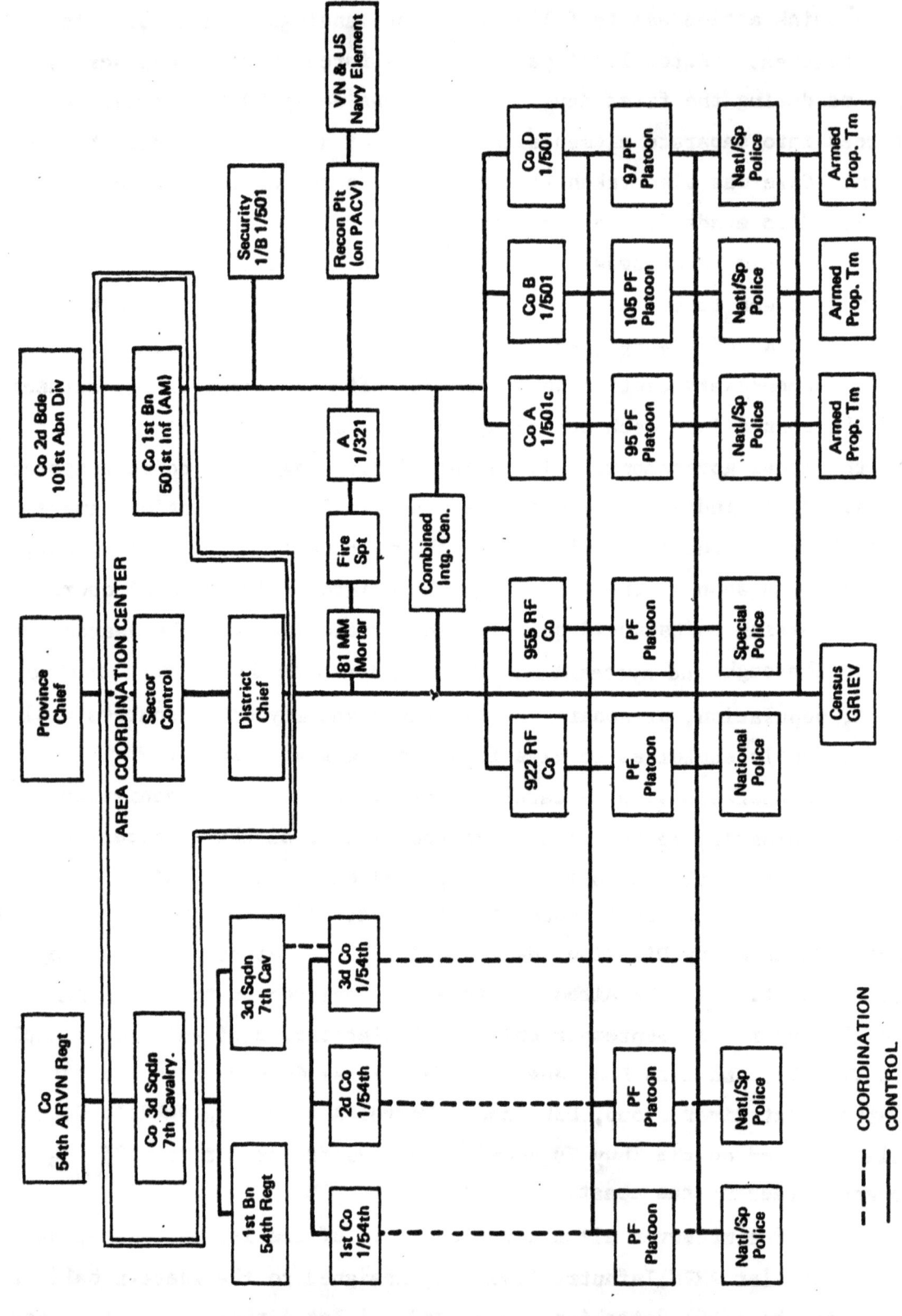

CHART 7—TASK ORGANIZATION, OPERATION LAMSON 260/NEVADA EAGLE

ARVN Infantry Division, assigned to operate with the 1st ARVN Battalion; 2 RF companies of Vinh Loc district, assigned to the center portion of the island; 3 PF platoons, assigned to operate with US forces in the eastern half; 100 National Police Field Force (NPFF) cadres of Thua Thien province; 8 census-grievance cadres of Vinh Loc district; and 17 police Special Branch, also of the district.

3. Control and special elements included: the 2d Brigade Command Group, located at Phu Thu; the 54th Regiment Command Group, co-located at Phu Thu; the 7th Cavalry Task Force Command Group, located in Vinh Loc; the 1/501st Battalion Command Group, located in Vinh Loc; the District Command Group, the Province Command Group, and the Combined Intelligence and Processing Center, all located in Vinh Loc. The Combined Intelligence and Processing Center was the most important of all elements. It was composed of the Provincial Intelligence Section, the Provincial Military Intelligence Detachment, the 1/501st Battalion S-2 section, the District Intelligence section, and the NPFF and Special Police Branch. In addition, special teams such as the Provincial Information Service team, and Provincial Psyops teams also participated in the operation.

During the night of 10 September, all blocking forces moved to their assigned positions. Most of these units were operating in nearby areas during that time. Thus their movements were made to appear routine and caused no suspicion to the enemy. Closing in stealthily by night, they were in position by the time the initial assault was launched. The cordon phase of the operation was a success; the enemy still did not suspect that he was trapped. *(Map 5)*

At 0715 hours on 11 September, elements of the 7th Armored Cavalry, which had embarked on naval ships during the night, landed at a beachhead on the western half of the island. They immediately pushed inland, dividing the island into two separate areas. This was the first time armored vehicles had been employed on the island; their presence, therefore, surprised and confused the enemy. Almost at the same time, the 1st Battalion, 54th Regiment, was helilifted into three assigned landing zones: Gray, Tan and White, on the western half of the peninsula. Two RF companies,

MAP 5. — OPERATION LAM SON 260/NEVADA EAGLE

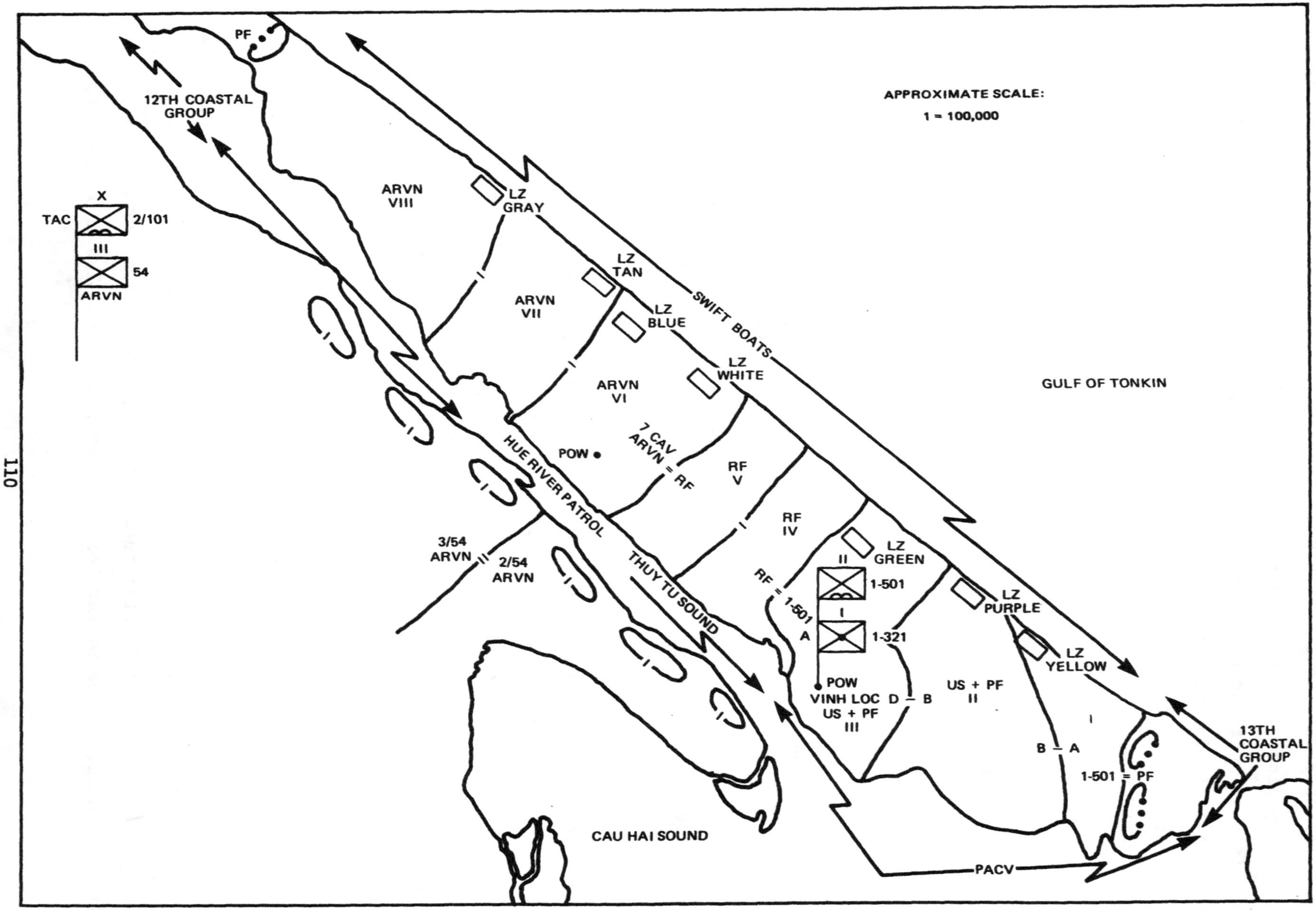

meanwhile, moved into positions along the beach in the center portion of the island. The 1/501st Battalion, as scheduled, alighted at three landing zones on the eastern half: Green, Purple and Yellow. By 1100 hours, all forces were moving southward across the island and by 1700 hours, they had swept through the last assigned targets located along the southern bank of the island.

During the first day of the operation, there were medium scale engagements with the enemy. Caught entirely by surprise, enemy troops did not have time to take evasive action or bury their weapons. They either surrendered or were captured. When the first day was over, more than 300 suspects had been detained. During the night, friendly forces consolidated their blocking positions and placed extensive ambushes over the avenues that the enemy might use to exfiltrate from the area. The entire island was illuminated by flares throughout the night.

On the second day of the operation, 12 September, friendly units began a careful search as they moved slowly back toward the sea. Each area of responsibility was minutely and methodically combed. During the operation, Vietnamese units proved their efficiency in thorough search techniques; patience was the key to their productiveness. As they continued the search, they made use of every bit of information provided by prisoners, returnees or the local population. Each source would accompany the search unit to the suspected area and guide our troops in their search. This method proved to be most effective and was used throughout the operation. Suspects were sent to the district headquarters where they were interrogated and screened by the combined intelligence elements. The interrogation and screening task was performed day and night, without interruption.

The heaviest engagement of the operation occurred on 12 September between US troops and the enemy. The 1/501 Battalion encircled the enemy C-3 local force company in an area about 2 miles east of the district headquarters. Caught in an open ricefield area, the entire enemy company surrendered after putting up a fierce resistance. Only 20 enemy troops succeeded in escaping the encirclement.

Throughout the operation, psywar activities were also pushed vigorously. Two loudspeaker teams accompanied friendly troops during the search. In addition, our aircraft flew many broadcast and leaflet-drop missions. The local inhabitants were urged to stay calm and not to be afraid of friendly troops. They were persuaded that once enemy installations and troops were destroyed, they would enjoy complete security under government control. These psywar activities proved to be effective in controlling the population and persuading several enemy troops to surrender.

Operation LAM SON 260/NEVADA EAGLE lasted ten days. By the last day, 20 September 1968, results obtained were substantial. The enemy lost 154 killed, 370 taken prisoners (including 126 VCI members, 155 guerrillas, 68 local force troops and 21 main force VC and NVA troops), and 56 returnees. A total of 1,970 suspects were detained and processed. Among them, 30 were found to be criminals; 55 were held for further investigation, and 139 youths volunteered for military service in the ARVN. According to one captured VC warrant officer, from 80 to 90 percent of VC cadres and troops in the island were killed or captured. The enemy was thus dealt a resounding defeat. Casualties on the friendly side were unusually light. Only one member of the propaganda team and one policeman were killed, and 12 wounded (7 ARVN, 3 US, 2 RF). Damages caused to the local population were also minimal: only 2 civilians were wounded and 3 grass huts were destroyed by fire.

Immediately after the completion of the military operation, a pacification program was initiated throughout the area. Two Rural Development teams had been brought in to Vinh Loc district on 18 September 1968, two days before the operation was terminated. Together with RF and PF units, they were assigned to organize local defense and re-establish local administration. At the same time, People's Self Defense teams were also activated in every village and hamlet throughout the district.

The local population of Vinh Loc district were greatly encouraged by the happy turn of events. They were all determined to return and rebuild their villages. In particular, they expressed the desire to see US and ARVN units continue their activities in the district until security became total. They requested very little assistance and relief from the district government, except for medicine and corrugated iron sheets for roofing. The district of Vinh Loc recovered rapidly under government control. Market places and schools were repaired rapidly and the local economy regained its normal prosperity within a few months. Afterward, the people of Vinh Loc district lived in complete security under the effective protection of popular and self-defense forces. This situation was maintained throughout the following years until the very last days of the RVN.

Some outstanding lessons were learned from operation LAM SON 260/NEVADA EAGLE. First of all, it was recognized that the policy of minimizing damage and casualties to the local population worked to the advantage of friendly troops and the government. This is a principle that ought to be applied to any operation conducted in a populated area. Fewer casualties and less damage means less burden for the government and less misery for the population. There is more cooperation with operating troops when it is realized that they come to protect and not to destroy. The LAM SON 260/NEVADA EAGLE operation succeeded because all commanders operated under this principle and took extra precautions.

The participation of provincial civilian and para-military forces proved to be very beneficial in this operation. Information concerning enemy whereabouts was instantly exploited and used. Also, there was less confusion and fear among innocent detainees. Local self-defense forces were employed to assist in searching their own villages. In the operation, 20 SDF members were helilifted to a search area where they effectively assisted US forces in rooting out the VCI.

The combined interrogation center functioned effectively and provided valuable information to operating forces. Its success hinged on good organization, continuous operation, instant exploitation of sources and innovative ideas. On 12 September, for example, a total of 212 suspects were routed to the center at one time. Their processing took less than two hours. Instead of lengthy interrogations, the police officers simply asked them to move to one side if they belong to the K-4 Battalion, and to the other if they belonged to the C-118 Company. Sixty-three among them instinctively did as they were told, thus, unwittingly giving themselves away.

The outstanding success of the operation, in general, was attributable to the excellent performance of all operational elements and to careful planning and close coordination. All participating commanders proved to be cooperative and determined to attain the common objective. Constant consultations and a perfect coordination of all efforts helped solve all misunderstandings. The key factors here were unity of purpose, integration of efforts, and physical proximity of control headquarters. What was more important though was the fact that no single element ever tried to claim all the credit for itself. It was a genuine combined effort in which the results obtained were a credit to all, regardless of who actually did what.

Flexibility in execution is another factor of success which should be regarded as a rule. The responsibility for exploiting information should be given to whichever unit is nearest to the target, regardless of boundaries or area of responsibility. A unit whose area of responsibility is unproductive should be immediately redeployed to where it can perform. Whenever a need for consultation arises, unit commanders should make an effort to get together. Also, supplies, information and other resources should be distributed on an equal basis and based on true requirements. All these factors were regarded as key to success in combined operations of all sizes between US and ARVN forces.

The 54th ARVN Regiment that participated in this operation was activated just after the 1968 Tet offensive. Its cadres and troops were relatively inexperienced. But this regiment proved to be able to perform just as well as any other that is properly motivated and led. During operation LAM SON 260/NEVADA EAGLE, this regiment made remarkable contributions in destroying enemy units and uprooting his infrastructure. It was subsequently redeployed to Nam Dong valley and participated in combined reconnaissances in force with units of the US 101st Airborne Division. Even in a different environment, it continued to perform well. The conclusion was that once the first step had been taken in the right direction, success could be expected to follow.

CHAPTER V

Combined Operations as a Means of Improving ARVN Combat Effectiveness

Objectives and Procedures

One of the major goals of MACV in South Vietnam was to help the RVNAF improve their combat effectiveness so that they would eventually be capable of defending their country unaided. The combat situation in South Vietnam offered excellent opportunities to put this policy to work since both the RVNAF and US Forces fought the same enemy on the same battlefield. The theory espoused by MACV was that, by participating in combat operations hand-in-hand with American units, Vietnamese forces—regular and territorial—would acquire valuable and practical experience which could hardly be acquired in a training center. Thus, combined and joint operations offered ARVN units not only the chance to observe American methods of operations, American use of firepower and mobility assets, and American leadership in action, but also offered the fringe benefits of additional combat support which could not otherwise be made available from Vietnamese resources. This was in fact a very special type of on-the-job or in-action training in which US units performed the role of instructor by giving real life, positive examples of combat actions and counteractions in various tactical situations and types of terrain; and the ARVN units under their tutelage benefited from observing and emulating the US units.

During the period of US active participation in Vietnam, this training concept was put to use at different levels and at different times. In late 1965, the III Marine Amphibious Force in I Corps Tactical Zone took up the most extensive organized effort of upgrading Popular Forces in a program called "Combined Action" which eventually absorbed a considerable amount of Marine manpower. Under the Combined Action Program (CAP), Marine rifle squads were sent into hamlets where they lived and operated with the local

Popular Forces platoons for a period of several months until the PF platoons were considered effective enough to defend the hamlets by themselves. The program was initiated at first around US bases and along National Route 1, then expanded outward until local security had improved to the degree that the Marines were no longer needed. At this level, the program was tremendously beneficial to the GVN pacification effort. As a matter of fact, it was the district chiefs who designated target hamlets for the CAP in accordance with pacification objectives and local conditions. Despite the fact that the program achieved remarkable success, it was not pursued on a country-wide basis since, unfortunately, it required considerable US manpower. Considering its achievements, one may wonder what the CAP would have contributed to the overall pacification effort, had the program been made a systematic and continuous combined US-RVN endeavor throughout the country. It was understandable that US forces were primarily concerned with destroying enemy main forces but it was also important to eliminate the enemy infrastructure which was at the root of insecurity. The commitment of US forces in this effort would have been entirely justifiable. Similar types of effort were made by US Army units elsewhere since 1965 but were not systematically continued due to the priority given to combat operations.

General Westmoreland felt that Saigon, the national capital, and its surrounding districts should be given priority in the common military effort since they involved the prestige of the GVN. The ARVN and territorial units which were assigned for the defense of this important area, therefore, should also be made effective. As a result, he directed, in late 1966, the initiation of Operation FAIRFAX, the first large-scale combined effort ever attempted, in which American and Vietnamese battalions were paired and tasked to support pacification in three key districts of Gia Dinh province surrounding Saigon. It was General Westmoreland's desire that US battalions, by participating in combat operations in a populated center, would inspire ARVN regular and territorial units and instill confidence among the population. The three participating US battalions were able to provide considerable combat support resources for the operation since they were subordinate to three different US infantry divisions.

Operation FAIRFAX, which lasted the entire year of 1967, was initially troubled by coordination and control problems. US and ARVN units, as a matter of fact, operated more on the basis of cooperation and mutual respect under the control of the district chiefs involved. Since the district chiefs, who were company-grade officers, were outranked by both US and ARVN unit commanders and not usually held in high regard by the latter, problems were bound to occur. In the absence of higher command directives, minor issues frequently developed into major problems. This situation changed for the better, however, when the 5th ARVN Ranger Group and the US 199th Light Infantry Brigade took over and assumed responsibility for the conduct of the combined effort. Coordination and control became more effective and the operation was termed a success when the US 199th Light Infantry Brigade was redeployed in November 1967 leaving only Ranger and territorial forces in charge.

After the enemy Tet offensive in 1968, combined operations of this type became more common. In principle, ARVN units remained under Vietnamese commanders although their headquarters were frequently collocated in the same base with US counterpart units. There were many cases, however, where small units such as platoons or squads were exchanged or cross-attached between US and Vietnamese units. In I Corps Tactical Zone, Lieutenant General Richard G. Stilwell, the new XXIV Corps Commander, went a step further when he suggested the integration of all US and ARVN tactical operations in his area of responsibility. His idea highly inspired me, who, as commander of the 1st ARVN Infantry Division at that time, was his counterpart. Jointly, we began to conceive operations and each of us contributed his share of the forces. Our units acted in concert under a virtual unified command since both of us were always in perfect harmony. We also encouraged the collocation of US brigade and ARVN regimental command posts in the same fire support base, since we were agreed that this provided closer and better coordination in tactical matters. General Stilwell was an indefatigable, energetic and devoted field commander. He and I usually worked very closely together and spent most of our days in the same helicopter visiting our units. It was my privilege to have been afforded the opportunity to cooperate with him

and earn his trust. Our association was truly a working relationship
inspired by the professional interest shared with each other and was in
contrast to the superficial politeness that characterized so many other
similar relationships. And I think that our joint efforts brought about
results which highly benefited the common cause we pursued.

The practice that we adopted was fully supported by Major General
Melvin Zais, Commander of the US 101st Airborne Division, who succeeded
General Stilwell in 1969. He applied similar methods along the same line
in the 1st Marine and the Americal Divisions. The Americal Division,
however, had for some time conducted combined operations with the ARVN
2d Infantry Division. The marked improvement of this unit's effectiveness
was largely due to these combined operations. The success achieved by
the Americal Division could be ascribed to its practice of establishing
common tactical areas of responsibility for both US brigades and ARVN
regiments and collocating their command posts at the same base camp.

In II Corps Tactical Zone, a combined operations program was initiated by Lieutenant General William R. Peers, commander of US I Field Force
in early 1968, with the cooperation of his counterpart, Lieutenant General
Lu Lan, Commander of ARVN II Corps. With the US 4th Infantry Division
guarding the central highland approaches, Generals Peers and Lu Lan began the "Pair off" program which combined forces of the US 173d Airborne
Brigade and the ARVN 22d and 23d Infantry Divisions. This concept was
later expanded to include Vietnamese artillery and other combat support
units. There were some drawbacks, however, in operational coordination and
cooperation due to the considerable separation of the Headquarters of II
Corps and I US Field Force and the relative lukewarmness of participating
ARVN field commanders.

In III Corps Tactical Zone, similar efforts were later made by the
commander of US II Field Force, Lieutenant General Julian J. Ewell. In
mid-1969, General Ewell, in cooperation with Lieutenant General Do Cao
Tri, Commander of III Corps, initiated the Dong Tien (Progress Together)
program which paired the 1st and 25th US Infantry Divisions and the 199th
Light Infantry Brigade with the ARVN 5th, 25th and 18th Infantry Divisions

respectively. Combined operations were most extensively conducted by the 1st US and 5th ARVN Infantry Divisions, and prepared ARVN units to assume almost all of the 1st US Division area of operation when it was redeployed in 1970. On the border areas, II Field Force paired Vietnamese Airborne brigades with those of the 1st US Cavalry Division (Airmobile). In time, the ARVN Airborne units became proficient in heliborne operations thanks to the large resources and modern methods used by US units. The Dong Tien program proved invaluable training for ARVN units which later successfully conducted the cross-border operation into Cambodia without significant US support.

Combined operations programs, conceived as a means of improving ARVN combat effectiveness, were a successful training vehicle. Not only did ARVN units improve markedly and became more proficient in modern warfare methods, but ARVN leadership also became more aggressive as a result of the fine examples displayed by US field commanders. In retrospect, these programs truly paved the way for Vietnamese commanders to assume new responsibilities as US forces began to withdraw. In contrast, combined operations certainly were not all crowned with success. There were difficulties and problems generated by human and procedural factors. The association with US units and their abundant resources also developed certain psychological conditioning and habits among ARVN unit troops and commanders which proved to be adverse in the long run. For the purpose of this monograph, the author proposes to examine in detail each of the four above-mentioned programs.

The Combined Action Program

Shortly after their landing in I Corps Tactical Zone, the Marines began a pacification program in the populated areas near Da Nang. The key to this program was the combined action concept whose basic premise was that rapport with the local population was both a military necessity and a prerequisite for permanent security. The problem of winning over the allegiance of the rural population was one of the most difficult challenges of the war, not only for the government of South Vietnam but also for the US forces who came to its assistance. This was a unique and unprecedented problem for American tactical commanders. Traditionally, American military doctrine, tactics, and training were geared to fight a conventional war; and little thought had been given to the political and psychological aspects of the type of war fought in South Vietnam, where many battles took place in the very midst of the rural populace. To overcome this problem, the approach employed by the Marines was to seek rapport with the rural population through the Popular Forces (PF), who were stationed throughout the villages and hamlets. Because these PF units were locally recruited, they enjoyed the advantage of knowing the local area and people, including the local enemy. In contrast, they were in general poorly equipped and deficient in leadership and training. These were deficiencies which could be overcome by US resources, leadership and know-how.

The method used by US Marines was to train by example, and the principle applied was to integrate a number of Marines at the lowest levels with PF units. The combined action concept thus was a happy marriage between two different elements who mutually reinforced and compensated for each other's weaknesses. In such an arrangement, PF units benefited from US firepower, communications with larger units, and medical evacuation. Conversely, US Marines were able to overcome some of the disadvantages of being foreigners.

The Combined Action Program started in August 1965 with a combined action company (CAC) composed of from three to twelve combined action platoons (CAP) initially assigned to the area around Hue city. It grew to 79 platoons grouped into 14 companies in 1967 and by November 1969, reached a total of 114 platoons grouped into 20 companies spread throughout the populated lowlands of all five provinces of I CTZ. *(Map 6)* These CAPs provided security for some 350 hamlets and protection for about 135,000 villagers. In manpower, the program involved about 2,000 Marines and Navy Corpsmen and approximately 3,000 PF troops.

Control and coordination headquarters for the CAPs existed at the District, Province, and Corps levels. The 114 CAPs were organized into 20 companies (CAC) which in turn were controlled by four Combined Action Groups (CAG). In general, company headquarters corresponded to and were collocated with District headquarters; group headquarters corresponded

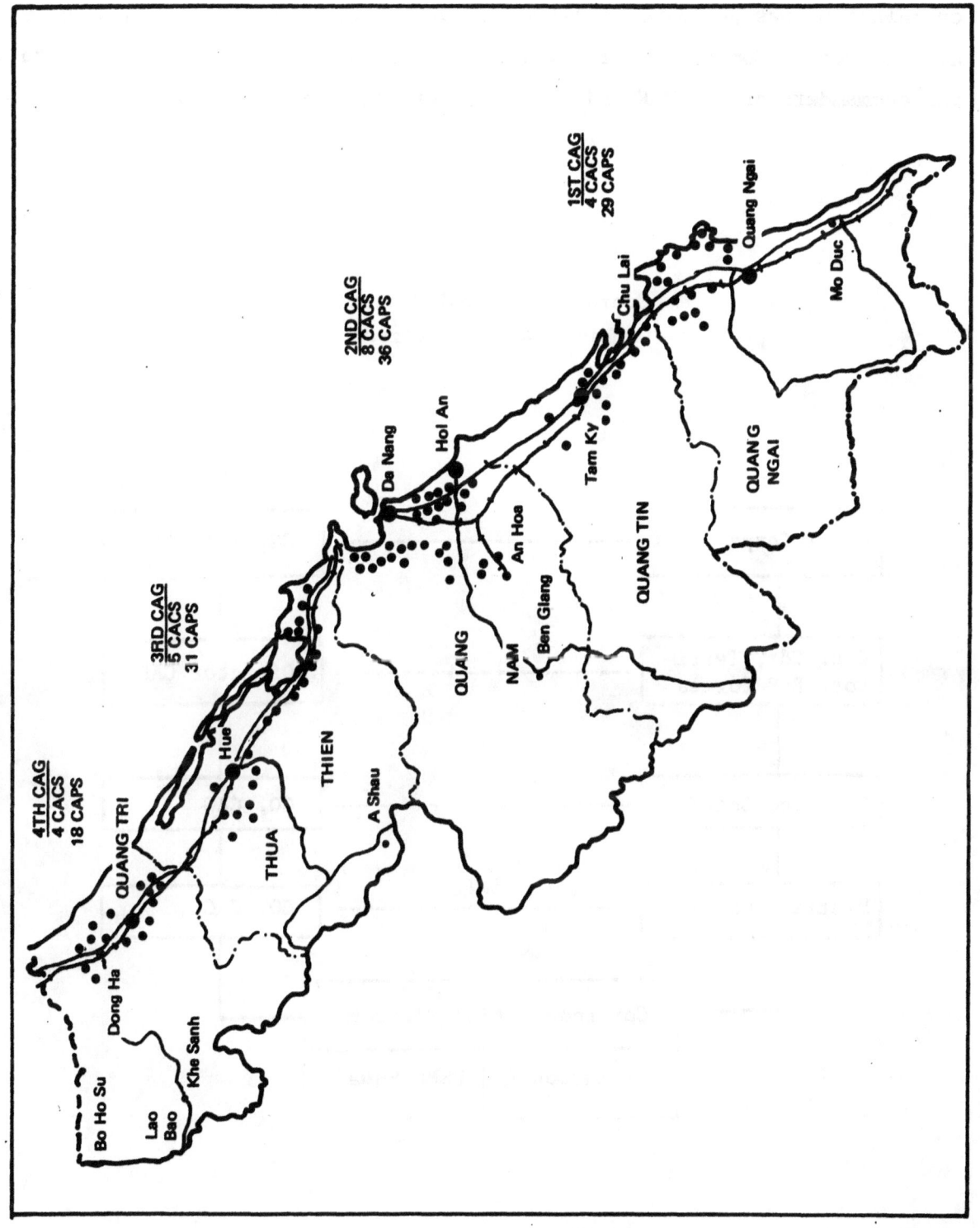

MAP 6. — COMBINED ACTION PROGRAM, ICTZ, NOVEMBER 1969

with and were usually located near Province headquarters. At Corps level, coordination was performed between the Director, Combined Action Program, and the Deputy Commander for Territory, I Corps, who in turn reported to the commanders of III MAF and I Corps, respectively. *(Chart 8)*

Coordination and Control
Combined Action Program
(Chart 8)

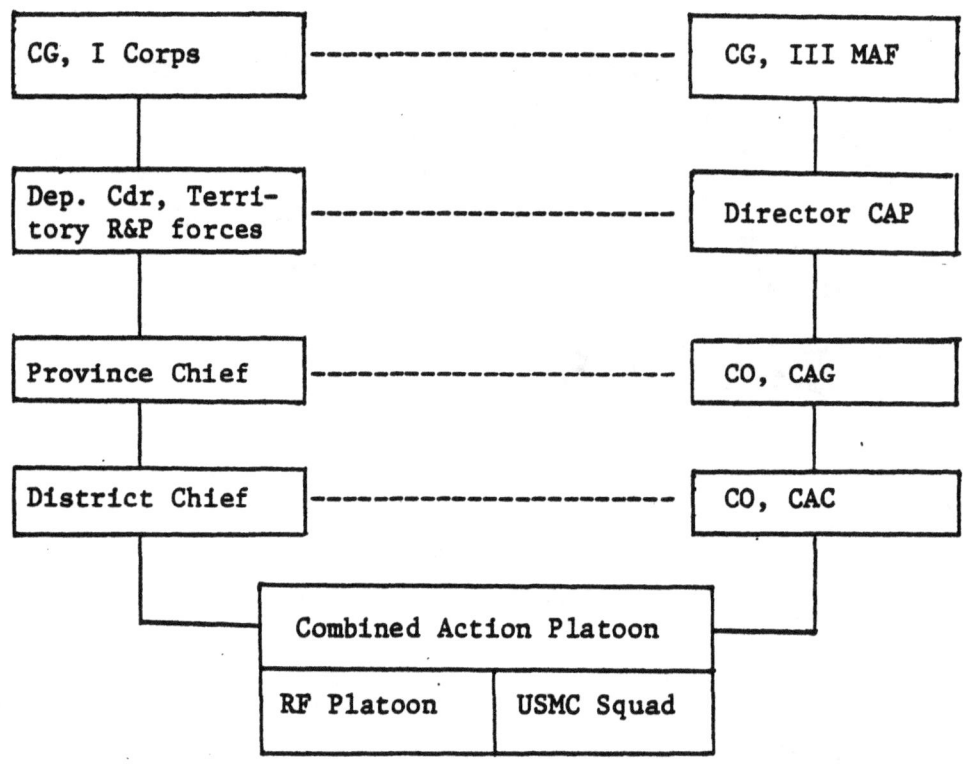

Basically, each Combined Action Platoon was composed of a USMC squad and a PF platoon. The USMC squad had 15 men, including the squad leader, 1 grenadier, 1 corpsman and 3 fire teams of four Marines each. The PF platoon, in theory, had 35 men, to include the platoon leader, a headquarters of 4 men and 3 rifle squads of ten men each. In total, the aggregated strength of a CAP was 50 men (15 USMC and 35 PF). In practice, however, the PF strength was never fulfilled due to various manpower problems encountered by the GVN. Initially, the CAPs were placed under operational control of the Marine commander of the tactical area of responsibility in which the CAP operated. In time, however, since the Marine element lived and worked with the PF and pacification being the primary mission, CAPs were placed under operational control of the local district chief.

Both the Popular Force and USMC elements of the Combined Action Platoon were assigned the following mission:

1. Destroy the enemy infrastructure within the village or hamlet area of responsibility.

2. Provide military security and help maintain law and order.

3. Protect the friendly governmental structure.

4. Protect bases and lines of communication within the village and hamlets by conducting day and night patrols and ambushes in the assigned area.

5. Contribute to combined operations with RF, ARVN, FWMAF and other PF units in the assigned area.

6. Participate in civic action and conduct psychological operations against the enemy.

7. Participate and assist in rural development to the maximum extent possible, consistent with the accomplishment of the foregoing tasks.

In addition, the US Marine element had the mission of providing military training to the PF troops in order to prepare them for more effective performance of their tasks when the Marines were relocated to another area.

Almost all Marines participating in the Combined Action Program were volunteers assigned directly from the US. A few volunteers came from III MAF units. Regardless of their origin, all Marines were screened for adaptability to the program; after selection, they attended a two-week CAP school at Da Nang before going to their CAGs for subsequent assignment to the CAPs. Some Marines later came back for intensive Vietnamese language training at Da Nang. Perhaps the foremost requirements for adaptability to the problem were the willingness to undergo hardship and above all, an affection for the Vietnamese people. In all frankness, we had to admit the cold fact that not all Marines—and US troops by extension—understood and warmed to the local Vietnamese people. While it appears doubtful that as many as 40% of the Marines disliked the Vietnamese, as claimed by a knowledgeable author, the fact was a Marine could not live and work with them unless he sympathized with and came to like them.[1] After all, this was a volunteer, not an assigned job, and a CAP Marine could quit any time he chose. The turnover rate, happily, was rather small throughout the entire duration of the program. There were even some CAP Marines who extended their tour of duty voluntarily for a period of three or more months.

A Combined Action Platoon was assigned to work with a village. Marines lived and worked with the PF in the village itself. They trained the PF in the daytime and, together with the PF, conducted patrols and ambushes at night. The headquarters of each CAP was a fortified compound consisting of several barbed wire fences, heavily sandbagged bunkers and a network of trenches. This was where the Marines and PF ate and slept, and worked in the daytime. The CAP headquarters was also a safe haven where the village chief and RD cadres sometimes spent their night. By any standards, living conditions in the compound were spartan: there was no electricity and no running water. At night about 6 Marines and 10 PFs guarded the compound, normally at 50% alert. The rest of the CAP

---

[1] F. J. West, Jr., <u>The Village</u> (New York: Harper and Row, 1972), p 11.

was out patrolling and laying ambushes. Patrols usually started at dusk and were conducted only as a means to drop off ambush squads or teams, generally two or three each night.

Tactics employed by the CAPs were founded on three basic principles: tactical mobility, economy of force, and credible permanence. Although a CAP did man and guard a headquarters compound, it did not defend the village or hamlet from behind bunkers and barricades. The basic tactical idea was to lay out a screen of ambushes on the approaches to the hamlet instead of putting up a static defense wall around it. The hamlet was usually manned by Popular Self-Defense Forces (PSDF). This kind of mobility was also used most effectively by the enemy. It instilled a psychology of offense, not of defense, and embodied, in practice, the precept of "defense through offense." Coupled with stealth, the kind of mobility practiced by the CAP provided not only offensive striking power, but also the protection afforded by elusiveness. By virtue of this quality of elusive mobility, the CAP seemed to be everywhere but never predictably anywhere. The unpredictability of CAP ambushes was the basis of CAP security against surprise attacks by overwhelming enemy forces and what was more important, it insured that the enemy would never feel safe anywhere in a CAP area of operations.

When a CAP first moved into an area, the Marines had to concentrate on basics and usually took a large share of the more dangerous duties. There always tended to be intense action and frequent contacts in the beginning before the enemy activity tapered off. Then the PF gradually took over, becoming more aggressive and more confident of themselves. Being a small element, the CAP, of necessity, had to apply the principle of economy of force. Its tactic was to combine a minimum of personnel with a maximum of firepower. In the presence of an enemy force, the CAP exposed only a small target yet was able to bring down the firepower of a Marine battalion in terms of air and artillery support. The CAP did not operate independently. Marine units usually conducted larger operations in the CAP's area, utilizing CAP personnel as guides and as a source of intelligence. These units also provided quick reaction forces to support the CAP in an emergency. In general, however, CAPs were capable of defending themselves against enemy local units.

The third principle of CAP tactics was that of credible permanence. The PF, being recruited from the local area, were villagers by nature. Like the PF, the CAP Marines were also villagers in that they lived with the PF and among the local population long enough to become known and befriended by the villagers. Their stay partook of permanence since they would remain as long as they were needed. In a sense, the CAP was practically "married" to the people, the village administrative structure, and the land. This quality of permanence was one of the characteristics that set the CAP apart from regular infantry units and accounted for its success among the local population. The CAP, as a secondary effort, also conducted civic action, not so much for what it could physically achieve with its limited manpower, but as a means of getting local officials involved in helping the people.

There was no question that the Combined Action Program had a generally good record. US Marines were fond of saying that no village under a CAP ever reverted to enemy control. That was true as long as the US protective shield was nearby. More meaningful, however, was the number of villages that ultimately no longer needed Marine protection. As a matter of fact, when Marines began to withdraw late in 1969, the security picture in I Corps rural areas was never so bright. The advantages of the CAP were obvious. It provided continuous protection to the village; it trained and motivated a local self defense force; and it was a potential source for the type of intelligence that would ultimately break the enemy infrastructure.

The presence of the CAP was a source of frustration to the enemy who attempted unsuccessfully to counter it. As a matter of fact, the enemy was able to destroy some of the CAP headquarters compounds by means of surprise attacks in force. But he never destroyed a mobile CAP. The effectiveness of the CAPs was demonstrated by the fact that wherever they were located, the enemy was denied his source of manpower because he was denied a free hand in recruiting and intimidation. The enemy was also denied his source of food since he found it too risky to run rice parties through the ubiquitous CAP ambushes. He was no longer able to collect his taxes of money or rice or enlist the support of the villagers. His source of intelligence gradually dried up as the villagers cooperated more fully with their PF and Marine protectors. Finally, the stability and credibility of the GVN was greatly enhanced when village officials could safely stay in their homes at night and the common people no longer feared reprisals from the enemy.

On the minus side, the CAP was costly in terms of American manpower. The Marines and the GVN wanted to expand the CAP, but MACV could not spare the manpower and instead developed the concept of Mobile Training Teams (MTT) to replace the CAPs. There were also difficulties in command relationship in some instances between the CAP and the local district chief. In one case, two village chiefs were summarily removed because they had received favorable publicity and eminence from close cooperation with US Marines. I Corps Tactical Zone was an area where local politics played a great role, chiefly at the district and village levels. The VNQDD (Vietnam Nationalist Party) and the Dai Viet parties had ramifications and influence among the population. Many able PF platoon leaders were dismissed or transferred because of their political affiliation, much to the chagrin of the Marines who only knew the military and professional aspect of the problem. After living a long time in the village, some Marines tended to become too independent and sometimes acted in defiance of their superiors. Fortunately, these cases of insubordination were few. In other cases, Marine energy and initiative tended to overshadow local Vietnamese military and civilian leadership whereas the real goal was to help these leaders become less dependent on American presence.

When the Americal Division took over the Marines area of responsibility in Quang Tin and Quang Ngai provinces in mid-1969, it continued the Combined Action Program with some modifications. The program was renamed Combined Unit Pacification Program (CUPP) although its basic concept was similar. The CUPP basic unit was the company whose squads were assigned to work with PF platoons like the Marines. But unlike the CAP Marines who were all volunteers assigned directly from the US and who stayed as members of a CAP for their entire tour, the Army squads which replaced them were not. Members of a CUPP unit were still part of an infantry company and continued to associate with it. The Marines employed the tactical mobility concept, without defense walls or perimeters. In the CUPP, hamlets were protected by a combination of a defensive perimeter and a series of nightly ambushes. In general, the Combined Unit Pacification Program, like the CAP, accomplished many of its objectives.

Operation Fairfax/Rang Dong

In late 1966 while the major American effort in III Corps Tactical Zone continued to focus on enemy main force units and American operations were typically large-scale efforts such as operations Cedar Falls and Junction City, General Westmoreland, commander of USMACV decided to commit an American infantry brigade on a long term basis to the Capital Military District which comprised Saigon and Gia Dinh province around it. This effort became known as Operation Fairfax which was initiated on 1 December 1966 and terminated on 14 December 1967. At the time of the decision, the security situation in Gia Dinh province was deteriorating rapidly and the enemy infrastructure and his 165A Regiment became a major problem. Many villages came under enemy control. The most troublesome areas were the districts of Thu Duc, Nha Be, and Binh Chanh, located directly east, southeast and south of Saigon, respectively.

According to General Westmoreland, the GVN was reluctant to put regular ARVN forces in the vicinity of Saigon and attempted to solve the security problem by increasing RF-PF strength. At his urging the JGS assigned two airborne battalions to CMD but their operations were ineffective. It was clear that ARVN forces could not cope with the situation. The GVN government, meanwhile, was just beginning its program of elections and its political stakes were understandably high. In the face of this situation, the USMACV commander recommended that US troops be committed as a catalyst for ARVN and RF-PF action. He advised the JGS that MACV would match one for one the three ARVN battalions to be committed.

In essence, Operation Fairfax was a combined operation conducted jointly by US II FFV, and CMD. "Rang Dong" was its Vietnamese counterpart code name. Forces deployed were three US battalions and three ARVN battalions.

The mission of Operation Fairfax stated that II Field Force, Vietnam in cooperation with ARVN/GVN would conduct operations in Binh Chanh, Thu

Duc and Nha Be Districts of the Capital Military District to destroy the Viet Cong forces, guerrillas, and infrastructure. *(Map 7)* The underlying objective behind this mission was the restoration of security in these areas to a level that could be maintained by ARVN, RF-PF, and the national police. The US battalions were also assigned the additional mission of training and improving the local RF-PF units to the extent that they would be able to provide continuing security after Fairfax ended.

Initial US forces committed to the operation were three infantry battalions, one from each of three US divisions: the 2-16 Infantry, 1st Division, the 3-22 Infantry, 4th Division, and the 4-9 Infantry, 25th Division. They were replaced in January 1967 by the US 199th Light Infantry Brigade. On the ARVN side, the JGS committed two airborne battalions of the general reserve, the 3d and 5th, and the 30th Ranger Battalion. These units were subsequently replaced by the 5th Ranger Group.

In the initial phase of the operation, the US 2-16 Infantry and the ARVN 30th Ranger Battalion were assigned to Thu Duc; the US 4-9 Infantry and the ARVN 3d Airborne Battalion were assigned to Binh Chanh; and the US 3-22 Infantry and the ARVN 5th Airborne Battalion were assigned to Nha Be. When the US 199th Light Infantry Brigade and the 5th ARVN Ranger Group subsequently took over, the 4th Battalion, 12th Infantry was paired with the 30th Rangers in Thu Duc; the 3d Battalion, 7th Infantry was paired with the 33d Rangers in Binh Chanh; and the 2d Battalion, 3d Infantry was paired with the 38th Rangers in Nha Be. Each US infantry battalion was thus collocated with a counterpart ARVN battalion and they shared a common area of operation which was the district. The 5th Ranger Group meanwhile detached a command liaison group to the 199th Brigade Forward CP at Cat Lai. This arrangement provided an effective coordination and command facility for the control of integrated operations in each district. To delineate areas of responsibility and to preserve basic unit autonomy, each district was divided into two TAORs, one under the responsibility of the US battalion, the other under the ARVN battalion.

MAP 7.— FAIRFAX/RANG DONG AREA OF OPERATION - 1967

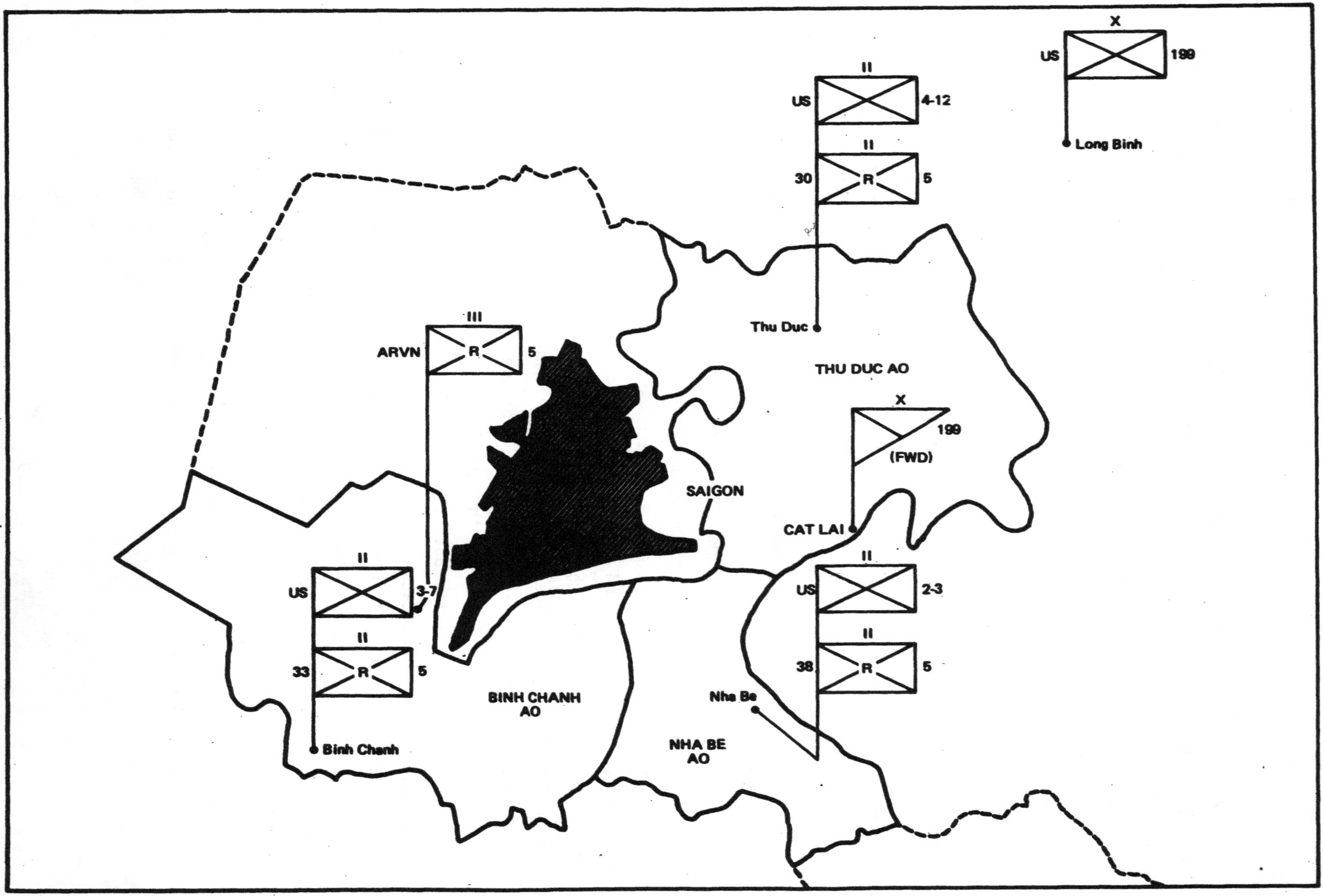

Since Fairfax was essentially a pacification operation, US and ARVN battalions were instructed to support the district chief and work for him. The rationale behind this was that operations would be no better than the intelligence provided by the district chief and he was in fact the government representative in the area. This cooperation was achieved through the establishment of an Area Security Coordination Council (ASCC) which was composed of the American and Vietnamese battalion commanders and the district chief. These principals met every few days to plan and coordinate the overall effort. The ADCC had no chairman or executive authority. All decisions were, therefore, based on mutual agreement or compromise. In essence, these meetings were the means of formalizing decisions before each of the three members issued orders through his own chain of command.

Other innovations in cooperation and coordination were the creation of a Combined Intelligence Center (CIC) and a Civic Action Coordination Center (CACC) which were in fact subcommittees of the ASCC and assisted the latter in matters concerning intelligence and civic actions. To motivate and gain the cooperation of the many different Vietnamese and American agencies involved, the US battalion S-2 served as the spearhead of the new combined intelligence effort which included the ARVN Battalion S-2, the district S-2 and Military Security Service, and the GVN combat police. The CACC was composed of the S-5s of the district and US battalion, the ARVN battalion and USAID representatives. The entire effort relied on voluntary cooperation. The CIC was in effect an attempt to organize a clearing house for the flow of various intelligence inputs. Its product was distributed to all members involved. Two helpful by-products of this effort were the creation of a combined interrogation section and a combined intelligence reaction force whose success greatly enhanced cooperation and enthusiasm.

The method of operation was a mixture of cross-attachment, pair-off, and integration. Since both battalions had four organic rifle companies, a company from each battalion was placed in direct support of the other battalion and vice-versa. The attached company was further broken down by exchanging platoons with the remaining two companies of the battalion. On many occasions, ARVN, RF, PF and US squads worked together. An additional area of emphasis was the requirement to provide maximum training to the district RF and PF units. This was accomplished by placing at least two PF soldiers in every American squad on a continuing basis.

The size of operations varied greatly. Several operations each month involved all eight rifle companies. On the other hand, combined platoons often conducted independent missions away from their parent units. Movement was by foot, helicopter and boat. While daylight operations were not normally smaller than platoon size, the basic unit for night ambushes was the combined squad. Under this system, the two battalions could saturate the district with over forty ambushes on a given night.

Specialized operations were also a part of the overall effort. Each week the intermixed units carefully cordoned and searched various villages in cooperation with district police forces. After several months experience and after the enemy main force units suffered heavy casualties, Fairfax forces shifted emphasis to small unit antiguerrilla tactics. This effort was a marked success. By breaking down into many small units and by moving constantly, the combined unit practically saturated the area of operation and effectively deterred enemy movement and resupply throughout the districts. Another tactic contributing to the success of Fairfax operation was the concentration of both day and night operations around selected villages identified as main sources of enemy subsistence. Also coordinated with saturation patrols and selective operations was the use of around-the-clock harassment and interdiction artillery fire and air strikes on the inaccessible enemy base areas which in fact drove the enemy either away from or into the area of infantry operations or into ambushes.

A movement control system was also initiated which designated certain key areas as off limits either to all movement, movement by sampans or motorized sampans, or movement without a special pass during curfew hours or even during daytime. Despite its military effectiveness, this movement control sometimes had to be suspended or modified in the interests of the local people who were in general farmers, workers, or merchants.

A training program for both the ARVN battalion and the RF-PF units went along concurrently with field operations. The battalion training program began at squad level and culminated in a battalion test administered by the American battalions. The three battalions of the 5th Ranger Group completed training in September and then were given a five-day concluding evaluation exercise. By November, all units were rated combat ready and as of December, the 5th Ranger Group assumed responsibility for military operations in the CMD with only a small US advisory element. To upgrade RF and PF units, US battalions tried a number of methods. First, there was a limited version of the Marine CAP concept. An American squad moved into a RF-PF outpost for a period of from two to four weeks. During the day, American and Vietnamese worked together to rebuild defensive positions using American materials following a joint plan approved by the district chief. In addition, the US squad gave weapons training and conducted practice firing. At night Americans and Vietnamese set up joint ambushes. Later the 199th Brigade formed Mobile Advisory Teams (MAT) which moved throughout the province assisting both RF-PF units and RD cadre teams.

Judged from the results obtained, there was no doubt that Fairfax operation was a success. It was the result of extensive planning and it received direct attention from the USMACV commander himself. The overall objective was achieved since security in Gia Dinh province improved remarkably. Over a thousand enemy were killed and 40 chose to return to our side. Enemy activity in general was severely disrupted although his infrastructure was not affected in any serious way. His efforts to reestablish his once-strong influence in the area surrounding Saigon, especially in Binh Chanh district, were largely negated.

The Fairfax operation lasted about one year. Over this period of time, it did produce a dramatic change, but a guarantee of long term results could not be expected. It generated a favorable mood of cooperation between US and ARVN units and also between ARVN units, the RF-PF, and the people. ARVN and RF-PF units performance improved markedly as a result of the example set by US battalions, their close association with the US battalions, the exchange of combat units, and the sharing of abundant American resources. They performed their mission well but were still not fully committed to the people. By contrast, US units developed good rapport with the local population, whom they zealously helped through civic actions. There were some reasons which could explain this apparent paradox. A major reason was that requests to assist the farmer, who probably lived better than the ARVN dependent, was not a reasonable demand in the ARVN soldier's eyes. Many of them wondered why they were not the ones to be assisted instead. Also ARVN units had very few resources with which to carry out civic actions. There were also the problems of ARVN leadership and discipline that probably would take a long time to be resolved and this depended on the dedication and examples of higher command leadership. In the special case of Fairfax, the US units proved that they could work well with the people and obtain their confidence over a period of time. The fine conduct of American troops perhaps was a backlash for their ARVN counterparts since it showed how differently they behaved.

On the negative side, first of all, there was no single chain of command. The ASCC was a good coordinating structure but did not provide for clear-cut command and control. Decisions were compromises between the individual interests of the US battalion commander, his ARVN counterpart and the district chief. The interplay of their personalities was the key to success. The critical factor in this arrangement was the district chief who was the junior in military rank, yet seemed to enjoy a greater power than the ARVN battalion commander. The CIC, although an excellent concept at the district level, was plagued by the scarcity of trained and qualified intelligence personnel. There was also the language problem which resulted in more time spent for planning, coordination, and execution and, not infrequently, in outright misunderstandings. The lack of interpreters at lower level combined units such as platoons and squads also impeded the joint effort to some extent.

In short, the Fairfax approach was not as permanent as the Marine CAP, and the relocation of US units was deemed somewhat premature. Here again, as elsewhere, American presence, initiative, drive, and resources were instrumental in gaining success, for a time. The permanent danger was that the ARVN had become psychologically and materially too dependent on Americans.

The Pair-Off Concept

The pair-off concept was instituted in II Corps Tactical Zone in the wake of the enemy 1968 Tet offensive as an offspring of the "one war" concept then embraced by MACV. Prior to this time, cooperation and coordination in II CTZ, in particular during the enemy offensive, was rather spasmodic and ineffective. The US I Field Force and ARVN II Corps usually operated separately, each concerned with and confined to its own responsibilities. While US forces sought out and fought enemy main force units in outlying areas of the central highlands, II Corps forces generally limited their activities to pacification support in the lowland coastal areas and populated centers. This was a reasonable division of tasks given the rugged and sprawling terrain and the relative ineffectiveness of ARVN units at that time.

It was then decided that since enemy forces, whether regular or local, were but one, the war effort should also be one. The key to success was now to exploit effectively the advantages of each national force while minimizing its disadvantages. To US forces, it was like fighting with blindfolds because the enemy was hard to distinguish. Hence, they preferred to keep to their own areas of operation. ARVN units, by contrast, knew the enemy and the terrain well but could not sustain combat for a lengthy duration, nor could they effectively plan and employ US combat support assets. Besides, accustomed as they were to the brushfire actions of pacification support, there was no way they could get off the ground and look the enemy main force units squarely in the face.

The pair-off concept thus came about as a means to upgrade ARVN combat effectiveness and prepare ARVN units for a larger share of the combat burden. It was decided that each ARVN unit was to be closely and continually affiliated with a US counterpart unit and that operations were to be conducted jointly, regardless of the size each force could commit. Coordination and cooperation were effected throughout the hierarchy from Corps to battalions and districts. Each month, the commanders of II Corps, IFFV and ROK forces and their staffs convened in a tripartite meeting during which the military situation was reviewed, problems discussed and resolved, and the objectives laid out for the following month in accordance with the

MACV-JGS Combined Campaign Plan. The three commanders took turns in chairing the meetings. Despite the great distance between II Corps and IFFV headquarters, located at Pleiku and Nha Trang respectively, Lieutenant General W. R. Peers, commander of IFFV made almost daily trips to II Corps headquarters. In addition, there were also periodic meetings of the various staff agencies of the three nations and daily contact and communications between them. Lieutenant General Lu Lan, commander of II Corps and Major General Choe, then Deputy, ROK Field Forces were in total accord with the pair-off concept. The "one war" concept pervaded the thinking and actions of all commanders and forces within II CTZ.

During the period of time the pair-off concept was implemented three significant combined combat operations were conducted almost simultaneously in II CTZ: BINH TAY/MACARTHUR in the Chu Pa foothill area, DAN THANG/McLAIN in Binh Tuy province, and DAN SINH/COCHISE in Binh Dinh province. *(Map 8)* Save for the Chu Pa campaign which was in effect aimed at destroying the NVA 24th Regiment in its base area, the other two operations were conducted primarily to assist the pacification effort in populated areas. The strategic objective of II Corps during that period was to expand government control of the population. Its efforts achieved spectacular gains by October 1968 when 95% of the population were reported living in A, B or C, i.e. secure, hamlets. The disposition and mission of each of II Corps major subordinate command was as follows: the 22d Division was supporting pacification in its area of operations (Binh Dinh, Phu Yen, Phu Bon) with emphasis on populous Binh Dinh province; the 23d Division, in an economy of force role, was conducting pacification and security operations in defense of major population centers throughout its vast area of operations (Darlac, Quang Duc, Lam Dong, Tuyen Duc, Binh Thuan and Ninh Thuan provinces); the 24th Special Tactical Zone was providing security in support of pacification in the populated areas of Kontum province, generally along National route QL-14; US forces under IFFV included the US 4th Infantry Division, headquartered at Pleiku, the 173d Airborne Brigade (separate) at Bong Son (Binh Dinh province) and Task Force South, a brigade-size unit at Phan Thiet.

PAIR-OFF II CTZ Senior Commanders Conference at Headquarters, IFFV in Nha Trang, July 1968. Sitting from left to right: MG Lu Lan, CG, II Corps; LTG William R. Peers, CG., IFFV; and MG Choon Shik Im, CG., ROK Forces, II CTZ.

DONG TIEN Joint Tactical Operations Centers, 1st Brigade, US 1st Air Cavalry Division and ARVN 2d Airborne Brigade, located in Tay Ninh, III CTZ, December 1969.

MAP 8. — PAIR-OFF OPERATIONS, II CORPS TACTICAL ZONE

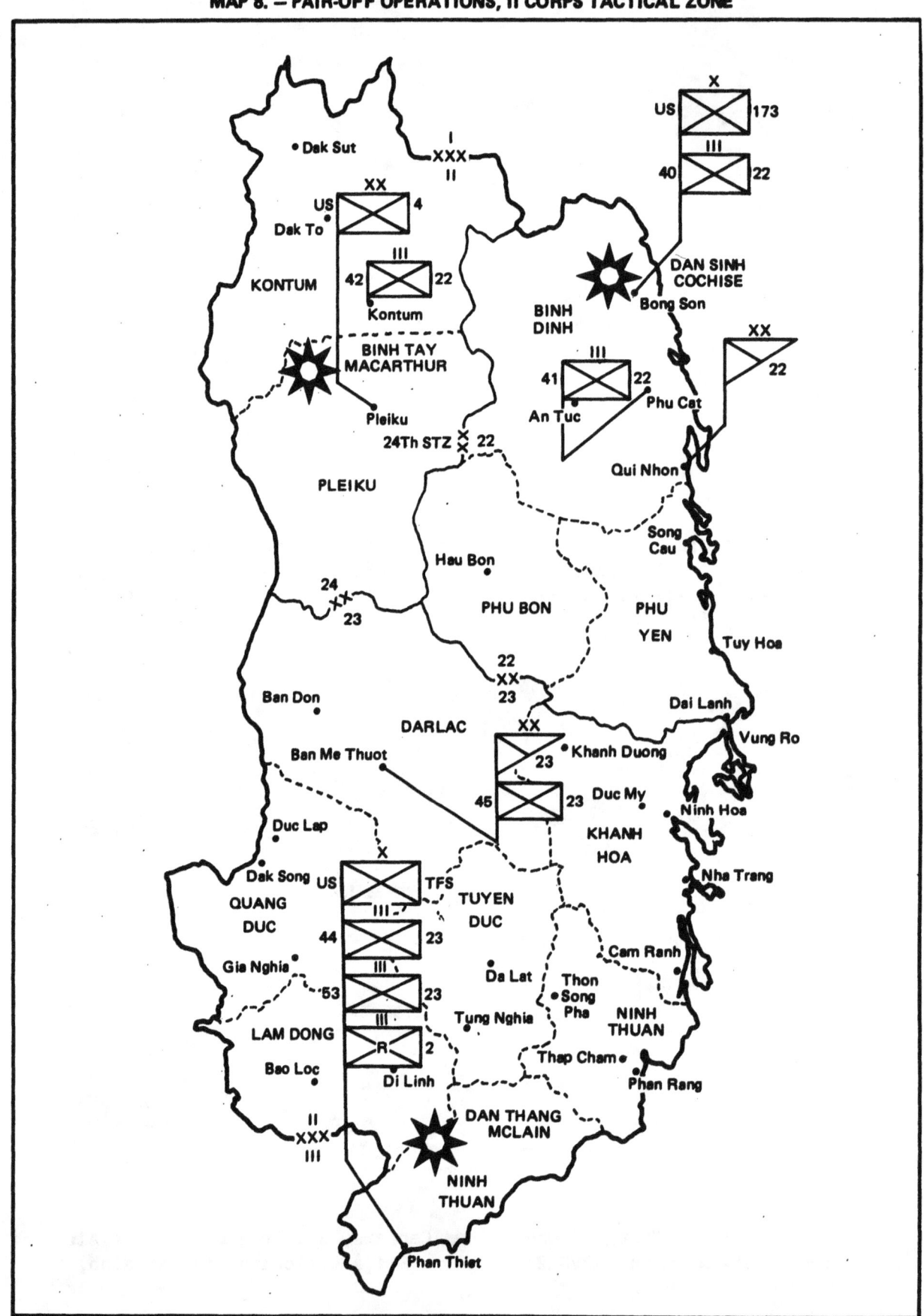

1. DAN THANG/MCLAIN Operation

This was considered the best example of the pair-off concept in action. Conducted on 1 August 1968, the operation combined forces of US Task Force South (2 battalions and 1 armor cavalry squadron) and those of the 23d ARVN Division (44th, 53d Regiments and 2d Ranger Group). The area of operation covered the northern part of Binh Thuan province and part of Lam Dong Province. The units collocated their command posts to simplify coordinating plans and operations. Bilingual operational plans and orders, situation reports, and briefings were used throughout. Combat support, including artillery, tactical air, and aviation was shared, based on tactical requirements. Of particular interest was the emphasis on naval gunfire support which was provided by the USS New Jersey for a six-day period in late October. RF and PF units were frequently integrated into operations and worked closely with ARVN and US units. In September, for example, one company of the US 3d Battalion (Abn) conducted a six-day combined operation with the 444th RF Company, including a combat assault.

During two multi-battalion operations conducted by the 3d Battalion (Abn) and the 2d ARVN Ranger Group, the respective command posts were collocated to facilitate coordination and control. The collocation of command posts and combined operations provided a good opportunity for ARVN troops, staffs and commanders to observe their counterparts at work in performing their respective tasks. This served to some extent to inspire our commanders, staffs and troops to learn by trying to do the same, but that was not enough. Perhaps, by operating alongside US units, they became more confident as a result of the lavish combat support they could obtain. But the most important result of the pair-off concept in this combined operation was increased and more sustained ARVN participation in combat operations. This, perhaps, was made possible by a combined effort at Corps and Field Force level.

2. DAN SINH-COCHISE Operation

Operation Dan Sinh-Cochise began on 22 August 1968 as a coordinated effort involving elements of the ARVN 22d Division and the US 173d Airborne Brigade (Separate). It was planned in three phases. Phase 1 was a search and clear operation to clear enemy forces from the operational area, northeastern Binh Dinh province. Phase 2 was a detailed search of the area including screening and classification of all the civilian population. Phase 3, a saturation phase, continued with US and ARVN forces operating in the area to deny the return of NVA-VC forces, to develop the confidence of the population in the government and ARVN units, and to protect the population from enemy harassment and exploitation. This operation was significant for two reasons. It was a completely combined and coordinated operation, at times involving three ARVN and three US battalions; it was also the first time US forces participated in a pacification support operation in a populated area of II CTZ, in keeping with the stepped up pacification effort.

 3. BINH TAY/MCARTHUR Operation

 This was a combined ARVN-US operation launched to counter the threat posed by the NVA 24th Regiment which was reported to have infiltrated in the Chu Pa mountains, northwest of Pleiku, toward the end of December 1968. The commander of the 24th Special Tactical Zone confirmed this information through a returnee. To preempt the enemy action, a combined operation was planned for January 1969 in the Chu Pa area. The mission was to defeat the enemy in the base area and to destroy his supplies. The operation was initiated on 4 January 1969 as battalions of the ARVN 42d Regiment on a reconnaissance in force mission began making daily contacts with elements of the NVA 24th Regiment.

 In the subsequent phase of the operation, ARVN battalions provided a blocking force while US battalions from the US 4th Infantry Division air-assaulted into the area and began sweeping in an effort to drive the enemy out of his dug-in positions toward the waiting ARVN forces. The operation ended on 28 February 1969 when the enemy withdrew into Cambodia. It was clearly a success since it preempted the enemy spring offensive in II CTZ.

 In addition to combined operations, a new advisory concept, designated the Combat Assistance Team (CAT) was formulated and tested by the Advisory Group of the ARVN 22d Division in August 1968. The test demonstrated that the proposed concept improved ARVN leadership and initiative and increased the ARVN capability for making independent use of US combat support assets. Accordingly, COMUSMACV granted each Corps Senior Advisor the authority to organize advisory elements under the CAT concept. Subsequent evaluation however, indicated that ARVN improvement was not as significant as anticipated, and that substantial advisory assistance was still required. In intelligence, under the pair-off concept, it was suggested by the Commander, IFFV, that each ARVN unit monitor should keep track of a specific VC unit but the idea proved difficult to implement. A substantial improvement was achieved, however, by ARVN artillery units as a result of the Associate Battery Program. US units provided survey data to ARVN units and assisted in the training of forward observers, fire direction center personnel, and gun section crews. Also, assisting the II Corps artillery advisor, were two artillery combat assistance teams (ACAT), one designated ACAT North assisting ARVN artillery units in the 22d Division tactical area and the 24th STZ, and the other ACAT South, assisting ARVN artillery units in the 23d Division tactical area.

There was no doubt that the pair-off concept, as seen through the above examples, brought about some measure of improvement and confidence among ARVN units. It was unfortunate that the program could not be sustained beyond 1969. Despite the temporary achievements, the fundamental, persistent, and most debilitating weakness of ARVN was the lack of strong leadership at all levels. US efforts to help ARVN forces overcome this problem were, in general, not too successful. Another weakness was poor and haphazard staff work, particularly at division and lower levels. This obviously stemmed from poor training and lack of demanding leaders. Coordination and cooperation, finally, depended on the examples set by higher levels of command. The problem was best summed up by Lieutenant General Lu Lan, commander of II Corps, when he said: "If at the top level, we don't coordinate, how do we expect coordination at lower levels?"

The Dong Tien (Progress Together) Program

Operation Dong Tien was a short-term test program which called for the close association of ARVN III Corps and US II Field Force units on a continuing basis in specific areas of III CTZ. It was a program jointly initiated by the commander of III Corps and the commander of II Field Forces. The program began on 1 July and lasted through the rainy season of 1969. Actually, it was somewhat open-ended with an underlying concept that as an ARVN battalion reached a satisfactory level of combat effectiveness, it was phased out of the program and returned to independent operations.

Three major goals that III Corps and II Field Force attempted to achieve through Dong Tien were:

1. to increase the quantity and quality of combined and coordinated joint operations;

2. to materially advance the three major ARVN missions: support of pacification, improvement of combat effectiveness, and intensification of combat operations;

3. to effect a significant increase in the efficiency of utilizing critical combat and combat support elements, particularly Army Aviation assets.[2]

Underlying these self-improvement goals was the objective of weakening the enemy at all levels so that on the one hand, his local forces could be controlled by the RF-PF and PSDF, and on the other, major ARVN and US forces could conduct combined and coordinated operations against NVA main force units in their base areas such as War Zones C and D during the dry season. To achieve this objective, the effectiveness of RF-PF and PSDF should be improved to the extent that they could assume the tasks being performed by ARVN units assigned to rural development and static security missions, thereby releasing ARVN units for mobile operations.

Within III Corps Tactical Zone, Dong Tien areas and associated ARVN-US units were assigned as follows: *(Map 9)*

Area	Province	ARVN	US
1	Binh Long and Phuoc Long	5th Inf. Division & provincial forces	1st Cav. Division (AM)
2	Binh Duong	5th Inf. Division & provincial forces	1st Inf Division
3	Long Khanh and Binh Tuy	18th Inf. Division & provincial forces	199th Light Inf. Bde
4	Phuoc Tuy	18th Inf. Division & provincial forces	1st Australian Task Force

---

[2] II FFORCEV Circular Number 525-1, 26 June 1969, jointly signed by Lieutenant General Julian J. Ewell, CG, II FFORCEV, and Lieutenant General Do Cao Tri, CG, III Corps and III CTZ.

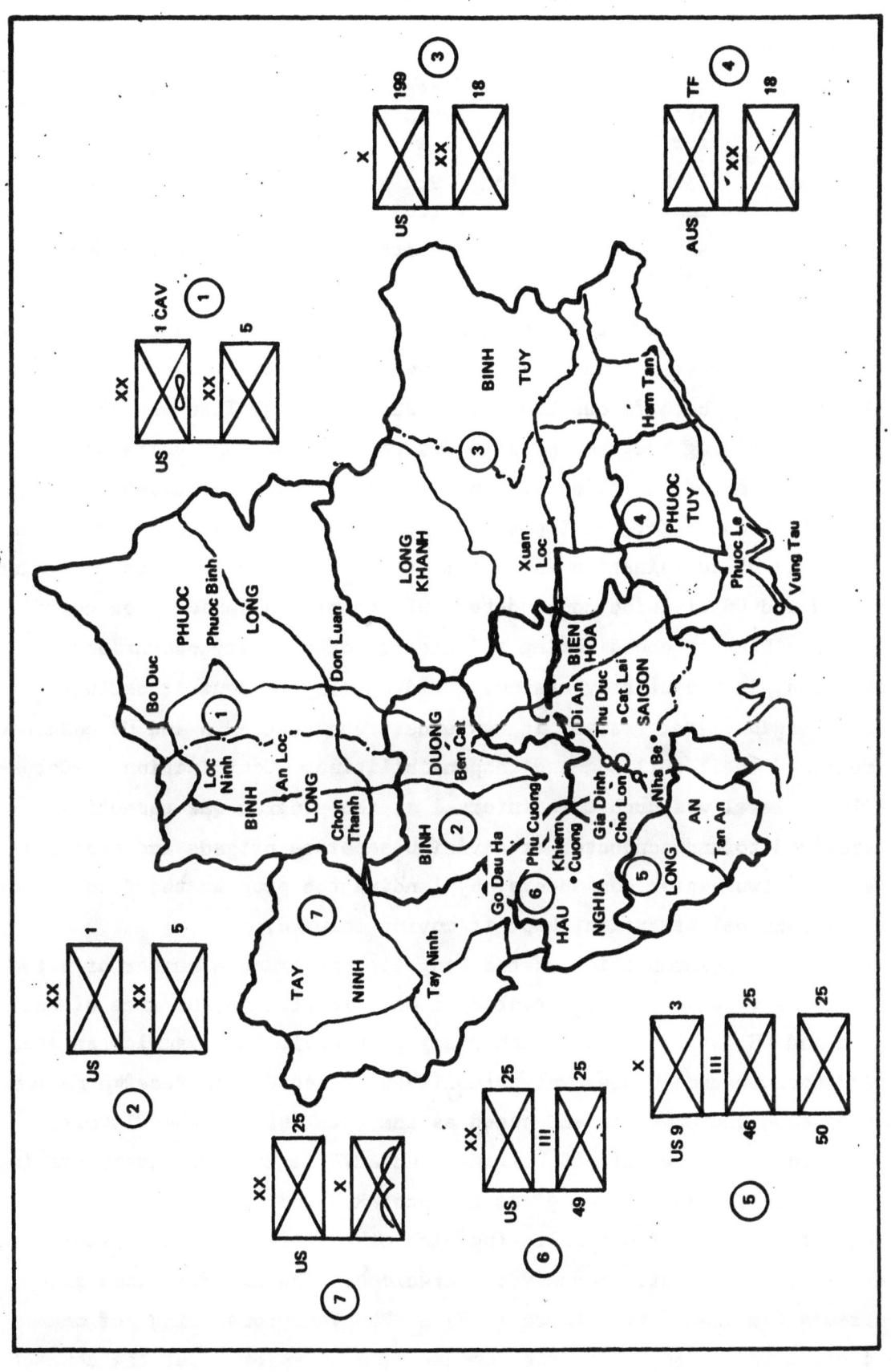

MAP 9.—DONG TIEN AREAS OF OPERATION, III CTZ

Area	Province	ARVN	US
5	Long An	25th Inf. Division (46th & 59th Regiments) & provincial forces	3d Bde, 9th Inf Division
6	Hau Nghia	25th Inf. Division (49th Regiment) & provincial forces	25th Inf. Division
7	Tay Ninh	ARVN general reserve units and provincial forces	25th Inf. Division

This assignment reflected no change in the deployment and disposition of ARVN and US forces. Dong Tien areas were the usual areas of operation to which units of both forces had been assigned. Dong Tien was also a short range training and test program designed to get ARVN units off the ground by the end of the rainy season. The procedures established by III Corps and II FFORCEV for the implementation of the program pointed to the usual formula of coordination and cooperation. In fact, in each Dong Tien area, ARVN and US division commanders would appoint a senior area coordinator responsible for coordinating all aspects of military operations. Coordination, it was clearly stated, would usually be done at sector/ regiment/brigade level. Also, it was understood that ARVN and US commanders each retained their full command responsibilities. Coordination at Corps- Field Force level was much more informal as the program was essentially decentralized to and conducted at division-separate brigade and sector level. However, the two senior commanders, by lending the program the force of orders and their personal attention, kept it moving forward.

In actual implementation of the Dong Tien program, a number of methods of operations were devised and tested at each level. In the area of the ARVN 5th and US 1st Divisions (Binh Duong province), for example, an area Combined Coordination Center was established at Ben Cat to receive reports from both ARVN and US units and acted as the catalyst for the lateral flow of information between US brigades and ARVN regiments. Every evening a combined staff briefing was given to both ARVN and US commanders with counterpart staff briefings following each other. These mutual briefings ultimately led to jointly conceived operations. The two divisions also organized a Combined Strike Force (CSF) at Phu Van, consisting of one US and one ARVN company under the command of a US major. But the concept did not work and the CSF was disbanded.

FAIRFAX Operation, Gia Dinh province. An integrated US-ARVN combat team heading back to base camp after an all-night ambush patrol.

DONG TIEN Commanders planning an operation (Left to right: Col. Robert Haldane, CO, 3d Brigade, US 1st Inf. Div.; Col. Le Nguyen Vy, CO, 8th Rgt., ARVN 5th Inf. Div.; LTC Maurice Price, Senior Adviser, 8th ARVN Rgt.; and Cpt. Chau Minh Kien, CO, 1-8 Battalion).

At regiment/brigade level, the usual method used was to collocate an ARVN battalion in the same Fire Support Base with a US battalion. Then the two battalions conducted planned combined operations from the FSB and in the area around it. In some instances, the ARVN battalion was prepared to assume complete responsibility for a certain FSB. In the FSB, the battalion TOCs might be either integrated, or combined or just collocated. Each of the methods used offered some advantages and the same number of disadvantages but the best was perhaps collocated TOCs. There were a few instances where units did not share the same FSB but cross-attached a liaison group at each CP. This was an arrangement which provided few advantages. In field operations, battalions usually used the method of the "dual company" with a combined CP, a method which offered the most advantages for the ARVN battalion. In the dual company method, platoons might or might not be cross-attached. In a few instances, companies were cross-attached in a battalion-level operation, but this was not an effective method since the ARVN battalion commander did not have the experience needed to handle a US Company. At the company level, platoons were usually cross-attached or they might operate as dual units. The same applied to squads.

In general, the dual concept appeared to work best at company level, since it offered an opportunity to develop the leadership capabilities of ARVN company commanders and at the same time provided maximum US support for the ARVN unit, while minimizing the loss of unit integrity. Combined with cross-attached platoons and squads, it was perhaps an excellent method to upgrade the combat effectiveness of the ARVN company, provided the two US and ARVN companies were associated on a continuing basis for a reasonable period of time. In terms of control and coordination, the collocation of CPs at battalion and company level was proved to be advantageous since it offered a maximum exposure to US staff and command procedures and maximum opportunities for coordination and cooperation. Disadvantages existed, however, in that ARVN commanders might be self-conscious of their own deficiencies and became dependent on US initiative.

The Dong Tien program definitely improved the combat effectiveness of ARVN units throughout III Corps although it was short-lived. The 8th

Regiment, 5th Infantry Division, for example, eliminated over 100 enemy per month in its area of operation, a threefold increase over the pre-Dong Tien period. As an ARVN unit showed definite signs of improvement, it was taken out of the program and assigned a separate AO of its own. The program's most eloquent result lay in the fact that, during 1970, III Corps units were able to successfully conduct independent operations striking into enemy base areas, and most particularly into Cambodia, with relatively little assistance from US forces. Many basic problems still plagued the ARVN at low level units, such as weak leadership, lack of planning know-how and the inability to effectively use combat support assets. In general, the better commanders benefited most; some of the others, while making progress, did not do as well. On balance, however, there was a general improvement in aggressiveness, better coordination, and more sustained combat effort.

Summary and Evaluation

Four different concepts and programs have been presented as approaches attempted by US forces to improve the regular ARVN combat effectiveness and upgrade the local RF-PF units. They have been selected over others for the reason that each effort was conducted in a different Corps Tactical Zone. Two of these efforts focused on low-level territorial units and took place in relatively populated areas. The two others, meanwhile, concentrated on regular ARVN units and took place in outlying areas. Perhaps the overall objective attempted by MACV when it directed and encouraged these efforts also encompassed a variety of purposes. This objective was reflected in its "one war" concept which purported, in effect, to be the answer to the enemy's "total war" and which was in line with the RVN strategy.

One of the key aspects of the Vietnam war that frequently escaped the minds of some military leaders was that it was a double war, one that was fought by main forces in a conventional manner, and the other waged at the grass roots level with local forces and guerrillas. The enemy was but one, whether one may choose to label him Viet Cong or NVA; he was the Vietnamese Communist, regardless of where he was born or trained. The arbitrary distinction between VC and NVA, however academically justified, was just a fallacy; and it served the myth perpetuated by the enemy that none of the NVA troops was in South Vietnam. The response to this double war was obvious; a double effort was to be made to eliminate the enemy at two different levels, in two different environments, and by two different approaches.

This was the rationale behind pacification and the upgrading of territorial forces on the one hand and the sharpening and strengthening of regular ARVN forces on the other. The strategy was both sound and necessary. All programs seemed to work for a certain time; their limited goals were all achieved, sometimes beyond expectations.

The Combined Action Program, for example, gave as good results as anyone could expect. It operated on the same tactical mobility principle of elusiveness that the enemy used so effectively. It presented a credible permanence that fostered the kind of popular rapport and allegiance that was needed to defeat the enemy's own kind of "people's war." It was finally instrumental in bringing about a strengthening of our own infrastructure while denying the enemy the very environment in which he usually prospered.

Discontinuing the program in favor of the less expensive MAT program seemed not to be well justified. What did two or three thousand Marines, or even more, really cost in terms of manpower as compared to the hundreds of thousands committed? There is little doubt that the CAP program was a positive influence and that the MAT program was less effective. One can only assume that US authorities felt they could not afford the personnel resources to implement CAP on a nation-wide basis.

The Fairfax operation achieved practically the same results as the CAP program, although on a smaller scale. Its success was made possible perhaps due to the personal attention of COMUSMACV himself. Besides, Saigon was an area of great importance to everyone concerned. "It must succeed," was the only explanation the COMUSMACV gave. The pair-off concept in II Corps CTZ, meanwhile, was not as successful as expected, perhaps because it came about too belatedly and was not sustained for a longer period. The terrain was rugged and too large even for the combined forces of three nations. Cooperation at lower levels was lukewarm at best, given the lack of interest at division level.

The Dong Tien program, by contrast, was a more complex enterprise which succeeded remarkably despite its few months of existence. The dual and cross-attachment arrangement at lower levels seemed to be the answer to the problem of effective cooperation and coordination. But it attested to the infeasibility of joint command at these levels, given the natural tendency of every ARVN leader to be his own boss.

Association with and exposure to US methods and initiative, however, brought to the surface many ARVN inherent weaknesses and deficiencies. Some of them were just differences in methods, culture, or way of life. Others were either technical or procedural problems that could easily be disposed of by more specialized and intensive training. Still others were human and difficult to resolve in the short term. The key to success in every human endeavor is of course people. In coordination and cooperation, personalities played the dominant role. Unless both commanders were willing to play the game and forsake their interest to a degree, there was no way to foster a genuine working relationship. Americans were usually impatient with ARVN lethargic work habits. Given their one-year tour, it was understandable that they always tried to get the most out of it. Vietnamese, meanwhile, felt they had all the time they needed. After all, they might well spend the rest of their lives with this war.

Poor planning was one of the most glaring ARVN deficiencies. It was even more acute at regiment and battalion levels. Perhaps lack of training was responsible for it; perhaps the quality and limited number of personnel available at these levels did not permit effectiveness in staff work. But the primary reason, however, seemed to be the lack of aggressive and demanding commanders. ARVN commanders at these levels, it was usually admitted, fought battles without tactics, relying primarily on their own personal methods. In addition, the ARVN commander was everything in the unit. His staff had little, if anything to say. It was the commander who decided every thing, told them what to do, where and when to go, and how to run the complete operation. And when he was absent, very little could be accomplished.

Finally, it was widely accepted that leadership was a perennial problem for ARVN at every level of its hierarchy. This problem was so extensive and so deeply rooted that it is difficult to explain thoroughly within the scope of this monograph. Suffice it to say that unless a commander or leader had professional competence, devotion, and moral rectitude, he certainly could not expect his subordinates to be dedicated and aggressive. The basic ingredients that were usually found lacking were: motivation and aggressiveness. Perhaps the passive and resilient nature of the Vietnamese could not produce the all-pervasive, gung-ho type of tigers of whom Westerners were so proud. In the context of an ideological conflict, there were certain other qualities that perhaps counted more in the eyes of the Vietnamese, qualities that were more ethical, more spiritual in nature. Perhaps lack of political awareness, and the social and economic degeneration due to the war were at the root of the problem, too. Whatever the causes, the problem certainly could not be solved in a year or two. There was finally the will and determination to fight, which again depended on motivation and leadership, and without which there was no sense in upgrading mere physical capabilities.

CHAPTER VI

Some Considerations Affecting RVNAF Performance

Expansion of the US Territorial Advisory System

As the pace of the US combat force build-up quickened after 1965, the advisory effort also expanded and developed at a rapid tempo. It was a dual effort by the United States to help build stronger regular forces to combat enemy main force units on the one hand and to assist South Vietnam to consolidate its governmental base so that effective control could be exercised throughout the national territory on the other. These two objectives were closely related. As has been said in the previous chapter, the war in Vietnam was a dual war which had to be fought on two different levels by two different approaches. While the destruction of enemy main force units required large-scale operations and the deployment of sizable units and resources, the task of helping South Vietnam consolidate its government demanded that security be provided at the village and hamlet level. Concurrently, as security improved, an expansion of the RVN influence and control was deemed necessary. These are areas where US advisory and assistance contribution were most beneficial.

The US involvement in South Vietnam began soon after the 1954 Geneva Accords with an advisory effort but this effort existed only at the highest level, in training centers and in major units. It emphasized primarily training and helping the ARVN reorganize its units. In 1959, when the military situation began to deteriorate, advisory teams were sent to infantry regiments and separate battalions in the combat arms of the Army such as Artillery and Armor, and in the Marines. The mission of these teams was to provide immediate assistance and also to evaluate the effectiveness of the advisory effort. Infantry battalions were assigned advisory teams for the first time in 1961. Also at that time each province was assigned a US adviser whose mission was to assist the province chief and sector commander in administrative as well as tactical duties. This new interest in territorial matters was perhaps due to the fact that the Civil Guard and Self-Defense Corps began to develop substantially during that time. Then in 1964, in an effort to effectively help the government of South Vietnam exercise control over the entire national territory, provincial advisory teams were increased and a limited effort was made to expand the advisory system down to subsector or district level during April and May 1964. This expansion was not systematic, however; it was designed to test the feasibility and efficiency of the advisory effort at that level. In the initial stage, MACV assigned only thirteen advisory teams, each composed of an officer and an enlisted man, to districts surrounding Saigon. After just one month of trial, there were definitely encouraging signs of success. As a result, 100 additional teams of five men each, including two officers, were rapidly deployed to selected districts during the period from September to December of the same year. During the next two years, 1965 and 1966, additional advisory teams were made available and by the end of 1966, almost all districts throughout the country enjoyed the presence of an advisory team.[1]

As of 1966, in view of the rapid expansion of territorial forces, MACV organized Mobile Advisory Teams (MAT) to work with RF and PF units at the village and hamlet level. By 1968, the US territorial advisory system was well established and functioning as a comprehensive and elaborate organization at the province level. *(Chart 9)*

The primary mission assigned to advisory teams at province or district level was:

1. To advise and assist the province chief or district chief and his staff in all matters pertaining to the counter-insurgency effort, the pacification and development program, and the operation of a military campaign.

---

[1] In some provinces and districts, US Special Force teams acted as advisors.

CHART 9—ORGANIZATION, PROVINCE ADVISORY TEAM
MARCH 1968

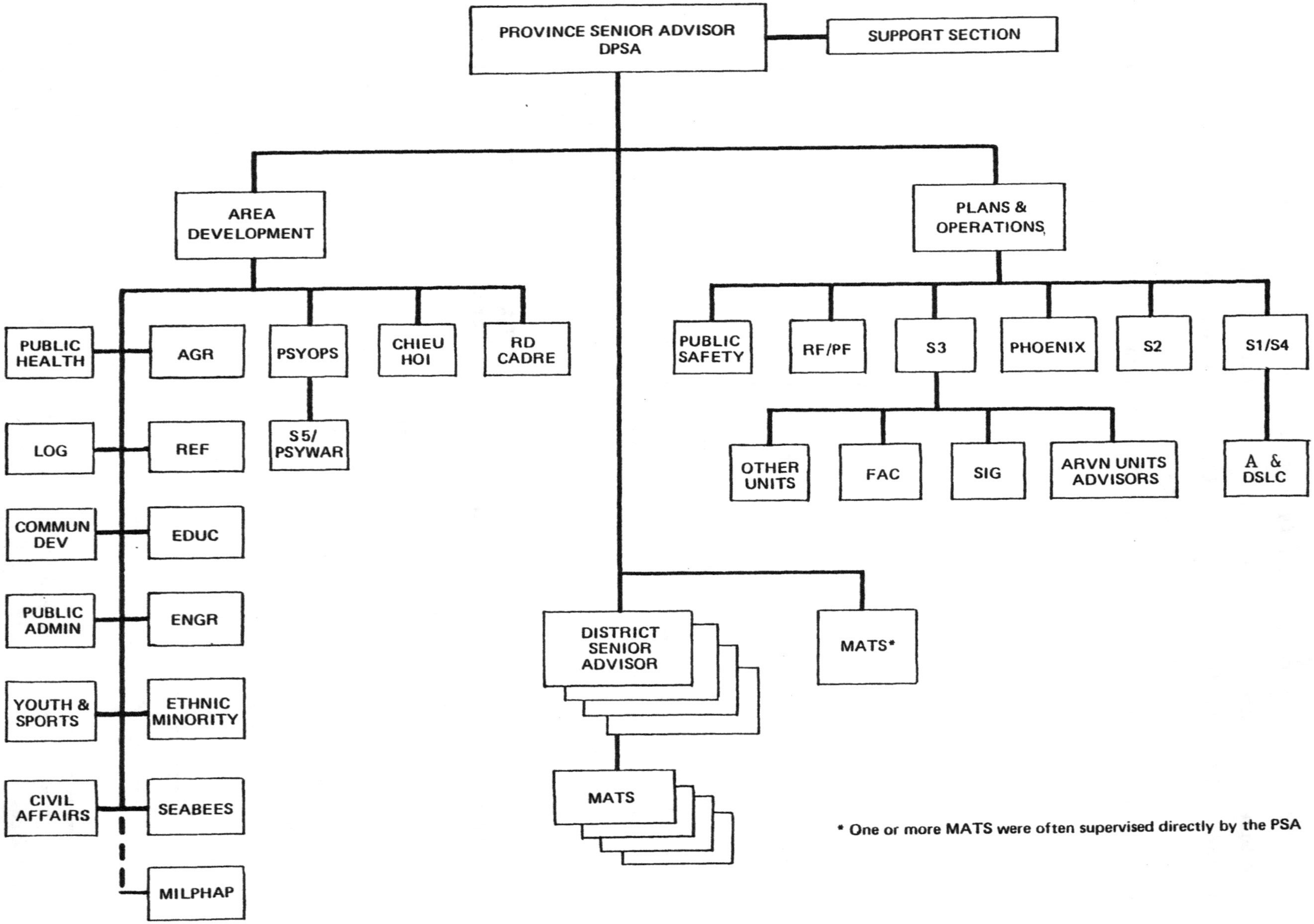

```
                         PROVINCE SENIOR ADVISOR
                                  DPSA ──────── SUPPORT SECTION
                                    │
            ┌───────────────────────┼───────────────────────┐
            │                       │                       │
      AREA DEVELOPMENT        PLANS & OPERATIONS      DISTRICT SENIOR ADVISOR
            │                       │                       │
                                                           MATS

   AREA DEVELOPMENT branches:
     PSYOPS ── S5/PSYWAR
     CHIEU HOI
     RD CADRE
     AGR ── PUBLIC HEALTH
     REF ── LOG
     EDUC ── COMMUN DEV
     ENGR ── PUBLIC ADMIN
     ETHNIC MINORITY ── YOUTH & SPORTS
     SEABEES ── CIVIL AFFAIRS
     MILPHAP (dashed)

   PLANS & OPERATIONS branches:
     PUBLIC SAFETY
     RF/PF
     S3 ── OTHER UNITS ── MATS*
        ── FAC
        ── SIG
        ── ARVN UNITS ADVISORS
     PHOENIX
     S2
     S1/S4 ── A & DSLC
```

* One or more MATS were often supervised directly by the PSA

2. To assist US and ARVN regular units located in the area or coming from other areas in the fulfillment of their mission.
3. To provide liaison between US units and the province chief or district chief and his staff.

By the very complexity and nature of advisory duties at the province or district level, there was a need to integrate the military and civilian effort in the advisory team. As a result, territorial advisory teams consisted of both military and civilian personnel who were selected among those more experienced in military and administrative matters. The composition and strength of each team, however, depended on security and political requirements of each particular locality. This afforded flexibility in organization and a more efficient use of advisory personnel. As a rule, if the senior adviser was a military officer, his deputy was a civilian and vice versa. At the district level, however, since their mission was heavily oriented toward territorial security, most senior advisers were military officers.

What frustrated the advisory effort most at the territorial level was the poorly-organized, under-staffed Sector (Province) or District headquarters. The lack of qualified and capable cadres in these staffs was a serious handicap. A Sector headquarters was authorized a strength of 183, including 32 officers, if the aggregate strength of RF and PF units in the province was more than 10,000. A Subsector (District) headquarters was only authorized 38 men, including nine officers, if the total strength of PF units in the district was more than 1,500. It was obvious that at the province level, the Sector headquarters was barely able to control and effectively employ a force whose strength approximated that of a division. As a result, RF and PF units were generally poorly led and ineffectively employed in the all-encompassing tasks of providing territorial security. This ineffectiveness gradually eroded the confidence of the local population.

Contrary to the usual uneasiness that Americans felt, the presence of US advisers in provinces and particularly in districts caused little adverse psychological impact among the population. Conversely, it was this American presence that created confidence in and prestige for the local government. Through the devoted advisory and assistance effort, many of the basic needs of the population were usually met and territorial forces were kept in fairly good shape. US territorial advisers usually spent half of their time on civilian affairs and the rest was devoted to the military effort. In this regard, military advisers provided very effective assistance to Sector and Subsector headquarters. Their contributions were particularly significant in the implementation of defense and of pacification and development plans, as well as in operations and in the employment, training, administration, and logistic support for RF and PF units.

As a result of this advisory and assistance effort, territorial command and control became more effective and the operation of Sector and Subsector headquarters became more systematic and efficient. Combat and logistic support for RF and PF units also had fewer problems. At the district level, the advisory effort was even more beneficial; it helped bring about a more rational distribution, employment, and control of RF and PF resources. In general, US territorial advisory teams were tremendously useful and efficient in problem-solving and rooting out inertia and complacency at Sectors and Subsectors. Particularly, in view of the language barrier and relative unfamiliarity of US personnel with local problems, the expansion of the US territorial advisory effort was a step in the right direction. Its achievements spoke for themselves. The improvement of RF and PF combat effectiveness, however, was an enormous task which required still more advisory effort and attention.

The Mobile Assistance Concept

The RF and PF were a sizable military force which made up approximately one half of the total RVNAF strength. They consisted mostly of companies and platoons scattered throughout the national territory with the difficult and important mission of providing and maintaining territorial security. The RF and PF soldier served in or near the hamlet where he was born and grew up. He was familiar with the natural and social environment and the situation in the locality where he was assigned to work and took an active interest in improving its situation. Basically, he was a good soldier endowed with resiliency and endurance. However, being part of the territorial organization, he was placed under an intricate command

and control system which generally inhibited his full development. As the lowest echelon in the military hierarchy, RF and PF units did not receive adequate training, equipment and support. Their effectiveness when compared with ARVN units was low; they usually came to be regarded as "poor cousins" by regular troops. Because of these inhibitions and constraints, RF and PF units seldom achieved a desired level of effectiveness. How, under those conditions, were they able to provide security and support for the pacification program, once US forces were redeployed and replaced by ARVN units? This was a major problem area that required a considerable effort of improvement if the RVN strategy was to succeed because half of the war was fought where the RF and PF were located.

Prior to 1968, there were no advisers with territorial units. As MACV viewed it, the assignment of advisers to thousands of units scattered throughout the country on a permanent basis was a difficult and costly proposition in terms of manpower and support. Any effort to upgrade territorial forces necessarily depended on the initiative and capabilities of US combat units operating in the locality; there was no other practical solution.

During 1967, US Field Force commands initiated an upgrading program for RF and PF units based on the mobile training concept. US Mobile Training Teams (MTT), each consisting of from three to ten members, were used in rotation among RF and PF units. The MTT mission was to organize, train, and supervise these units until their performance was deemed satisfactory. Various names were given to these teams and all indicated to some extent the nature of their mission. There were, for example, Combined Mobile Training Teams, Combined Mobile Improvement Teams, "Red Catcher" and Impact Teams, and Regional Forces Company Training Teams. The advantage of this mobile training concept was the ability to provide training for a large number of units within a reasonable time. But for that very reason, the time that a mobile training team was able to spend with each unit was necessarily limited; hence, the results achieved were also limited. Even with this economical use of training manpower, the mobile training program proved costly in US personnel because the number of RF and PF units had increased considerably. And when conducted separately, this training effort ran short of the close coordination and cooperation which were required for any combined effort to become a success.

During this period, the Joint General Staff also initiated its own programs for improving the effectiveness of territorial forces with the encouragement and assistance of MACV. Under these programs, RF companies were rotated between field duties and training. They underwent a 12-week training program at National Training Centers just like regular units. The advisory effort, meanwhile, turned to the organization of RF company training advisory teams which were test-deployed in all Corps Tactical Zones. Each team usually consisted of three officers and three NCOs and was attached to a RF company undergoing training at the National Training Center. Its mission was to assist in training the company. After the formal training program was completed, the team stayed with the company for a period from six to nine months to follow up on its training until the company was judged capable of independent operation. For all its merits, this method of training failed to bring about significant results.

Finally in late 1967, drawing from previous experiences, MACV initiated an extensive improvement program for territorial forces based on the Mobile Advisory concept which had been successfully adopted by II Field Force. This effort aimed at improving territorial forces in all aspects: tactical operation, administration, and logistic support. In addition to Mobile Advisory Teams, MACV also created Mobile Advisory Logistical Teams (MALT) whose mission was to help upgrade the territorial logistic organization and operation.

This large-scale improvement program was implemented in early 1968. A total of 353 Mobile Advisory Teams was planned and by year end, they had been deployed to all four Corps areas. Before their field deployment, these teams received training at the US Army Vietnam (USARV) Adviser School. Upon completion of training, they were assigned to provinces with the mission of upgrading RF and PF units by directly advising

and assisting their commanders. Each MAT consisted of two officers
(team chief and deputy), three EM (one light weapons infantryman, one
heavy weapons infantryman, and one medic), and one Vietnamese interpreter
The team usually lived with a RF and PF unit if the situation permitted.
Its members helped train the unit and accompanied it in operations.
Emphasis was placed on command and control, the conduct of operations,
particularly night operations, marksmanship, the use of mines and booby
traps, and the planning and control of fire support. After achieving
its goal of upgrading the territorial unit—which was usually done
within 30 days—the MAT moved to another unit and started the training
process again. From time to time, the team also revisited an old unit
to evaluate its progress and to provide assistance as required in order
to prevent the unit from deteriorating. A MAT sometimes worked with
a RF company and several PF units nearby at the same time. The success
of Mobile Advisory Teams could be measured by the improved capability
of the territorial forces to conduct independent operations with a
minimum of support from the outside.

During 1969, the MAT effort also assisted local governments in
expanding control, constructing more outposts in areas formerly under
enemy control, coordinating the use of fire support, and developing and
employing the command and control capabilities of RF Company Group
Headquarters. These were territorial tactical commands activated during
1968 under the control of Sector commanders. Each RF Company Group
Headquarters consisted of one commanding officer, his deputy, two officers
and three NCOs who made up three staff sections: operations, intelligence,
and training. The Headquarters was designed to exercise operational control over a territorial force of approximately five RF companies or an
equivalent number of PF platoons. By 1970, when almost all RF company group
headquarters and companies had achieved substantial improvement, the
MATs were redeployed to areas where village and hamlet security needed
to be improved, and where the local government control required consolidation. Their new mission focused on upgrading the Popular Forces,
training and deploying the People's Self-Defense Forces, and coordinating

A Mobile Advisory Team, 11th US Armored Cavalry, instructing the 948th RF Company, 1968.

Artillery Advisor and counterpart during drill

activities of Rural Development cadres and the National Police. The MATs also assisted in developing village defense systems which were realistically tailored to local requirements. As the situation and time permitted, the MATs also assisted, advised and encouraged village chiefs to initiate and implement village self-development programs.

After several tests and trials covering a long period of time, the MAT program was found to be the most effective and realistic instrument for upgrading the combat capabilities of territorial forces. An outstanding example of its success was the marked improvement brought to the great mass of RF and PF units in the Mekong Delta, a sizable but ineffective territorial force which had been plagued by lethargy and indolence. Although the task was enormous and complex, MAT members quickly adapted themselves to each situation, strove for innovative ideas and unfailingly fulfilled their responsibility. Their presence and assistance in the improvement of rural security brought confidence to the population and prestige to the RVN government.

The role of territorial advisers was challenging and interesting. In time, it became one of the most important contributions made by United States forces in South Vietnam. As long as the advisory effort lasted, it helped improve the image of the RF and PF trooper, who, like his communist adversary, could fight like a tiger if properly motivated and led, but seldom did because he was not.

Attitude of RVNAF Troops Toward Americans

The presence of Americans in South Vietnam no doubt accounted for the pervasive confidence among the population and RVNAF troops that final victory would eventually be theirs. As far as the RVNAF were concerned, Americans were either advisers, samaritans, or comrades-in-arms. This American standing prevailed no matter how ugly the Americans were painted by Communist propaganda. Very few people in South Vietnam were suspicious of American good will and altruism.

The American involvement had a good start in the mid-fifties when the US began to assist the development of the nascent National

Army of Vietnam. Its goal then as always, was to make South Vietnamese forces strong enough to defend their land and their people. It was realized that without a strong native army, South Vietnam could hardly defend itself against subversion and invasion from the north, regardless of how many allies came to its assistance.

During its first few years of existence as an independent republic, South Vietnam was able to stand firmly on its own due to American aid and assistance, which also helped it build a viable military force. Under the guidance, inspiration, and assistance of American advisers, this military force gradually developed into the full-fledged Republic of Vietnam Armed Forces, a source of pride and confidence for the nation. In Saigon, staff members of the US Military Assistance Command acted as advisers to their Vietnamese counterparts in the Joint General Staff in matters pertaining to intelligence, plans, programs, and operations. In the field, US advisers were permanently deployed to regular maneuver battalions and as Mobile Assistance Teams roving among territorial forces. In the initial stage of the war, however, these advisers were primarily concerned with the distribution of war materiel and the training in its handling and use. But when fighting escalated seriously, American advisers became increasingly involved in tactical and combat training for units and in advising and assisting unit commanders in the conduct of operations.

Despite its limitations in personnel, the advisory presence greatly influenced a unit's performance. With only a few members, US advisers did the best they could to take care of problems and they constantly strove to help make the unit effective. In addition to resources that they could make available for operational requirements, their knowledge of techniques, planning, and operations also contributed a great deal to the successful accomplishment of the unit mission in several instances. The unit commander also benefited in many ways. The presence of advisors acted in essence both as a catalyst that transformed and improved and as a stimulant that spurred and activated both the unit and its commander. As a result, command and control at every ARVN echelon became more effective and unit performance improved markedly.

On the other hand, the presence of advisers in several cases stifled the unit commander's initiative and downgraded his authority and prestige. As a matter of principle, an adviser exercised neither command nor authority with regard to his counterpart; the relationship between the two of them was necessarily based on mutual trust and respect. In almost all cases, the adviser simply acted as an assistant to the unit commander; in principle, he should restrict himself to that capacity. But there were instances that required the adviser to transcend his capacity and practically take over in the name of the unit commander. This occurred in a few units whose commanders were weak and indecisive in the face of combat pressure. The power and influence of US advisers in the field did tend to overshadow the role of Vietnamese unit commanders. For example, activities of a unit tended to follow along the lines recommended by the adviser. In many instances, it was the adviser who won the battle by calling in effective tactical air or firepower support from US resources. This gradually produced over-reliance and sometimes total dependence on US advisers. As a consequence, the initiative, responsibility, and prestige that the unit commander usually wielded were greatly affected and, over the long run, the presence of advisers resulted in reduced opportunity for ARVN cadres to develop their command capabilities and leadership.

When US combat units were introduced into South Vietnam to fight the war, their role overshadowed the advisory effort because they held the initiative on the battlefield and coordinated all military efforts. As of this time, ARVN units began to keep close contact with US units through the intermediary of advisers. Their purpose was to obtain additional support from US resources to meet operational requirements, and, almost unfailingly, US units obliged by giving all that had been requested. Because of the plentiful and sometimes lavish support provided by US units the morale and combat effectiveness of ARVN units was very high. Later when called upon to participate in combined operations with US forces, ARVN units appeared to enjoy the opportunity if only because of the dependable support they could always expect. In time, they came to regard Americans as protectors and providers instead of advisers and comrades-in-arms.

The consequence of over-reliance on material assets as substitutes for initiative and prowess was a failure to develop the infantryman's capabilities to the full—the very qualities that distinguished the Vietnamese soldier: endurance, perseverance, resiliency and manual dexterity. Because they were organized and trained by US standards, and exposed for a long time to US warfare methods, ARVN units inevitably became accustomed to conducting operations with an abundance of supporting material resources. The result was that when American presence and assistance were no longer available, the morale and combat effectiveness of ARVN units became uncertain.

The Tendency to Let Americans Do It All

The American military presence in South Vietnam, with its powerful combat forces, its impressive array of resources and its gigantic bases, really overshadowed the Republic of Vietnam Armed Forces. The Vietnamese people suddenly found their own military force shrunken to the size of a midget. There was nothing in the RVNAF comparable to the awesome might and modern assets which symbolized the "omnipotent" posture of the United States. Soon, they were convinced, Americans would deal the insurgency a resounding defeat. Those were the first impressions engendered by the initial buildup of US combat forces and their successful offensive campaigns to retake the areas that had been lost to the enemy. At that time the Vietnamese were reassured and, by staking total confidence in US might, they took little interest in the efforts of the RVNAF, which appeared in their eyes as insignificant and superficial.

It was true that even the highest field commands, the ARVN Corps, had only limited resources and limited capability. At best, they were just capable of controlling territorial security activities and implementing short-term plans such as dry season or rainy season campaign plans, and plans for the protection of rice crops, national resources, etc. Those were routine and undramatic plans which looked more important in form than in substance and which were renewed and repeated every year. Small wonder that nothing substantial had ever been achieved through such operations. Corps commands almost never deployed and operated in the field as tactical headquarters. They never had the opportunity nor the requirement to operate in the field because operations were usually conducted at the battalion or regiment level, or at the most and only rarely, at division level. And most operations lasted only a short time to allow units to return to their territorial duties to which they were permanently tied.

When US Field Forces began operation in Corps Tactical Zones, their capabilities and combat posture practically turned each of them into a key tactical command for the initiation and coordination of all military efforts within its area of interest. For one thing, Field Forces had a better grasp of the military situation and for another, almost all support resources were under their control. This operational practice reflected and befitted the realities of this period and was deemed vital for the integration of all military efforts to effectively counteract an emergency situation. From a temporary arrangement dictated by expediency, US Field Forces gradually became permanent. Their initiative, responsiveness, and all-pervasive efficiency soon stifled the development of ARVN operational capabilities at the tactical level. Soon, ARVN tactical commanders began to lose their combat initiative and became overly dependent on US forces for meeting major enemy initiatives. Gradually they lost interest in the combat situation outside of pacification areas. It was as if the war was being fought in a distant and alien world. ARVN commanders had little idea of what US forces were doing; US activities were after all none of their business. The passivity and lack of enthusiasm on the part of ARVN tactical commanders resulted in a greater freedom of action for US forces, first of all because ARVN units would not get in their way and second, if they were called upon to cooperate, there was not much they could contribute to the joint effort.

During the period from 1965 to 1968, ARVN units performed only a secondary role which was mostly confined to the support of pacification. US units, meanwhile, were responsible for nearly all combat operations throughout the Corps areas. The less spectacular operations of ARVN units earned them the unjustified criticism that they were not too concerned with the combat situation. In fact, there was little they could do about it. ARVN units had indeed improved a great deal in combat effectiveness by this time but they were still considered not up to the task of taking on major enemy units. In general, they were inadequately equipped to respond effectively to operational requirements. It was during this period that combined operations were initiated, but the idea of cooperating with ARVN units was not widely welcomed by US forces. In the eyes of some US commanders, ARVN units were but an additional burden they had to take in tow and that were apt to cause more problems than they were worth. Moreover, the feeling among some US commanders during that period was that US forces alone could defeat the insurgency without ARVN participation.

The strategy then adopted by MACV and the JGS concerning the prosecution of the war placed equal emphasis on three major tasks: combat operations, pacification, and territorial security, which were all equally important. The division of tasks, as outlined by the Combined Campaign Plan, was a judicious distribution of responsibilities in which each force, Vietnamese or American, was employed according to its capabilities or where its advantages could be best exploited. The attempted goal was to achieve a balance of tasks which could eventually bring about maximum contribution to the joint effort. Hence it was agreed that US forces, with their plentiful resources, would tackle the hardest part by conducting search-and-destroy operations while the lesser endowed ARVN forces focused their efforts on pacification and security. ARVN units accepted this division of tasks with some reluctance since most of them would have welcomed the opportunity to conduct mobile operations, especially when reinforced by American firepower and mobility support.

ARVN units at that time were seldom given the opportunity to develop their combat effectiveness, bound as they were to the tedious task of pacification support and territorial security responsibility. Boredom and routine gradually eroded their combat skill and spirit to the point that they became almost as passive and as lethargic as the territorial forces. But the enemy 1968 Tet offensive came in time to offer ARVN units the much-welcomed chance of undertaking active combat operations once again. Starting with the battles fought during this offensive, ARVN units really took the big leap forward and contributed a larger and larger share to the combat burden heretofore almost exclusively borne by US forces.

In the area of logistic support, much has been said about RVNAF lack of planning and overdependence on US resources. This was true to some extent because the RVNAF logistic system was more geared to area support than to mobile operational support. By and large, the primary supply requirements for area-type activities consisted of foodstuff (rice) and ammunition for small arms. These basic commodities were generally stocked in field depots at a level that provided continuous supply for several weeks, if not months. Field units usually drew their supplies from these depots by their own means. Rarely was a supply point established for the sole purpose of supporting a particular operation. Logistic planning therefore was not particularly emphasized throughout the hierarchy.

So when it came to providing support for large-scale, combined-arms operations which were conducted away from bases and lines of communication, the RVNAF logistic system usually ran into difficulties. Experience showed that combat units participating in these operations were in short supply for almost everything. The major obstacle was and had always been the lack of transportation resources. For such operations, logistic planning of necessity required a long time for preparation and for coordination with several different units. The risk of disclosure, therefore, was so great that operational commanders usually avoided detailed logistic planning for security's sake. Besides, the RVNAF did not have the resources nor the capability to effectively support major operational efforts, particularly when these involved the use of helicopters for supply and support. During the Lam Son 719 operation into Laos in May 1971, for example, it was the US forces that provided almost all of the logistic support for ARVN units. In other cases, US logistic support was needed at least during the initial stages of an operation so that it would not end up as a failure because of supply or materiel shortages.

The conclusion that has to be drawn from the foregoing is that if there really was a tendency to let Americans do it all, it was not the natural and common inclination of all ARVN commanders. But it did exist to some extent. Thus, either it could be attributed to undue reliance and uncritical confidence on US capabilities and resources, or it stemmed from a common desire shared by both sides to meet emergency requirements.

Effect of One-Year Tour and Six-Month Rotation

Hundreds of thousands of American servicemen contributed to the American effort in Vietnam over the years of involvement and direct participation. They either served in US units or as advisers to the RVNAF; there were many among them who volunteered for more than one tour of duty; some served two or even three tours. Except for the top positions, the usual tour of duty for the American servicemen in Vietnam was one year. It was a short time indeed, but for all practical purposes one year seemed reasonable enough and was suitable to most of them. The continuous exposure of US troops to field conditions and war risks, however, made the one-year tour of combat duties a long one, particularly in the Vietnamese environment. Hence a six-month tour rotation policy was adopted to alleviate trauma and risks. Since the American participation in the ground war was not designed to last for a long time, it was a reasonable policy to allocate the hardship so that nobody had to endure more than his fair share. This policy proved beneficial for the upkeep of morale and effectiveness, as far as US combat forces were concerned. For the advisory program, however, the one-year tour obviously had its drawbacks.

Among ARVN units, the change of personnel, particularly in command positions, greatly affected the performance of the unit. Because of the lack of a solid foundation and despite formal standing operating procedures, all activities of the unit depended almost entirely on the personality and capabilities of the commanding officer. If he was a good commander, the unit performed well. But if he was ineffective, the unit was apt to deteriorate rapidly. In contrast, US units appeared not to be affected much by personnel change. This was due to established traditions, a solid foundation and well-honed operating procedures from the top to the bottom level. A good US commander could only make his unit a little better whereas the worst that a bad commander could do to his unit was a slight decrease in overall efficiency, which in most cases was hardly perceptible.

Although the one-year tour and six-month rotation policy gave rise to minor problems of personnel turbulence and loss of continuity, it was beneficial in many ways. Due to established procedures, regulations and training, new arrivals in a US unit were usually able to familiarize themselves quickly with unit problems and have a "feel" for unit operations within a short time. The short and definite period of one year was an incentive that spurred them to give the best of their abilities and performance to contribute to the unit achievements. If the tour of duty had been longer or open ended, the protracted combat and hardship in an unfamiliar environment would certainly have worn them down and made them weary of the war effort.

The six-month rotation of battalion and company cadre between combat and staff duties was a judicious arrangement that improved the quality of performance in both duties. A staff officer with combat experience would certainly perform better than a desk-bound officer. However, for higher level command positions, a certain continuity and longer combat experience was necessary. Brigade commanders, for example, should have served at least one year in their position. It was obvious that familiarity with the unit and stability of command at these levels could tend to cushion the adverse effect caused by the quick turnover of personnel at battalion and company level.

Over the years of association with the US presence, each Vietnamese commander worked with several American advisers; they lived with each other and fought side by side like a man and his shadow. An ARVN commander usually stayed in his position for many years but every year he had to work with a different adviser. At the battalion level, this change in relationship occurred every six months. The relatively rapid turnover of advisers at battalion level had a definite adverse effect on the advisory program. While an adviser did not command the unit, his prestige and standing among ARVN troops were considerable. He was understood to be in a position of power and authority with regard to his counterpart. As a result, every change of adviser disturbed the atmosphere of the unit.

An adviser's duties necessarily required a minimum of stability and continuity. His activities were not confined only to the unit he advised; they also encompassed the total environment in which the unit operated. Consequently, the adviser had to perform in both capacities: military and civilian. Despite the fact that the advisory system was well established with time-tested procedures that enabled an adviser to acquaint himself rapidly with a new situation, he certainly had to rely on past experiences and knowledge in order to effectively solve many different and complex problems in his area of responsibility. A case in point was the District Senior Adviser whose tour of duty was extended to 18 months instead of 12 in later years. This extended tour not only benefitted the advisory system in terms of personnel stability, it also enabled the adviser to assist the territorial forces and the population more effectively because of his long experience and familiarity with the locality and its environment.

In contrast to the US combat serviceman, the adviser lived with Vietnamese soldiers and in close touch with the local population, both of whom had spent their entire lives in war. What they needed was someone whom they could trust and on whom they could depend throughout the years. The adviser's short tour of duty was certainly no help in this regard. The longer an adviser lived with a unit and shared the hardships and dangers with its men, the more the men in the unit felt close to and trusted him out of a sense of loyalty and confidence. The adviser's position also required him to have some continuity in his assignment in order to fully grasp every problem concerning the unit and the external influences bearing on it. This was the best way he could find the appropriate ingredients for improvement—by living and taking advantage of his experience, not by arbitrarily suggesting innovative ideas.

CHAPTER VII

Summary and Conclusions

The introduction of US combat forces in early 1965 saved the Republic of Vietnam from military defeat and helped it restore stability and consolidate a more viable regime. The short term goals that the United States set about to accomplish were successfully achieved within a relatively short time. Despite obstacles, the Americans also finally succeeded in developing and improving the Vietnamese armed forces on which the Republic of Vietnam depended for its survival.

Resorting to the use of combat force meant that the US advisory effort and level of military assistance up to that time had either fallen short of their goal or were not enough. Then three and a half years of intensive fighting also failed to bring the enemy to his knees. Entering the war with the posture and disposition of a fire brigade, the Americans rushed about to save the Vietnamese house from destruction but took little interest in caring for the victims. Only after they realized that the victims, too, should be made firefighters to save their own houses, did Americans set about to really care for them. Valuable time was lost, and by the time the victims could get onto their feet and began to move forward a few steps after recovery, the fire-brigade was called back to the home station.

Throughout the years of participation, the American presence greatly bolstered the RVNAF performance and morale. There could be no doubt about it. The position enjoyed by Americans with regard to the RVNAF was either adviser or comrade-in-arms. Well established and with carefully selected personnel, whose devotion and abilities were undeniable, the US advisory system admirably performed its difficult and complex role. American combat units also made substantial contributions to this effort.

It was obvious that, while operational cooperation and coordination between RVNAF and US forces might not be an ideal solution for the conduct of the common war effort, it was the most realistic way to improve morale and combat effectiveness of the Vietnamese armed forces. Cooperation and coordination also helped to make the task of US forces easier to carry out in many ways.

It is difficult to make an assessment of the US advisory effort. Suffice it to say that it was instrumental in transforming a disorganized, poorly-led, and unschooled army of some 150,000 into a modern and highly organized tri-service military force nearly ten times as large which successfully held and pushed back the NVA invasion of 1972. During the first few years the effort of US advisers met with considerable obstacles, particularly in the area of training. Several years of hard fighting on all battlefields from north to south and of living close to French forces—and undoubtedly under their influence—had instilled a certain psychology of intractability, unruliness, and complacency among the Vietnamese military cadre. Their adjustment to the American way of doing things was painful and slow. They found American training and warfare methods too inflexible, too mechanical, and not realistically adapted to the Vietnam battlefield. The language barrier and cultural difference also formed a wide and seemingly unbridgeable gap. To a certain extent, the Vietnamese were not interested in training and did not think it was necessary. After all, they felt they were experienced enough and knew how to fight this kind of war. American tactical advice was something they thought they could do without.

During the early sixties most US Army company-grade officers that were assigned to field advisory duties—except for a few Korean War veterans—had no combat experience. They were in a truly awkward position vis-a-vis the Vietnamese regimental and battalion commanders who had gone through so many battles during the first Indochina war. Their role and effectiveness, as a consequence, were greatly reduced. The adviser's duties were mostly limited to end use inspections, maintenance of weapons and materiel, and assisting the unit in military techniques and logistics, but seldom in operational matters. This situation changed, when US combat support assets—airlift, helicopters, and later, tactical air—were made available. For the first time, ARVN unit commanders felt vulnerable and helpless without advisers who controlled and provided the support assets. The role of advisers began to grow in importance and their effectiveness increased markedly with the advent of airmobile operations and US tactical air support. This new aspect and level of the war had changed the advisory relationship for the better.

The training and development of the RVNAF made encouraging progress as a result of increased US assistance and advisory effort. But soon these achievements were undermined by political events that began in late 1963 and carried into the next few years. Command and control of the RVNAF, which had for years been a basic weakness, were further disorganized and weakened by political intrigues and machinations. The armed forces were in deplorable shape and their deterioration prompted the United States to intervene. The experience of this period demonstrated that no matter how effective the military advisory effort might be professionally it could do little to influence the course of events unless the advisers to key command positions also doubled as political counselors. But the nature of the war and the realities of a developing country in which the military so strongly dominated politics perforce perhaps would have required a special breed of politico-military advisers.

If the RVNAF had had a tight and unified command system throughout the entire hierarchy—from the top echelon to the PF platoon—then the US advisory effort to develop and improve these armed forces would certainly have been much easier and less painful. For the Vietnamese private—whether regular or territorial—was basically a good soldier, courageous, enduring and resilient. The young cadre at low level units were also highly motivated, enthusiastic, and easy to mold. The trouble was that these fine soldiers and cadre were not brought along by good leadership. In general, the pressure exerted by advisers to relieve ineffective commanders or to withdraw from units with a poor record only worked at the lower levels. It served no practical purpose for the benefit of the RVNAF apart from causing confusion among the troops. In retrospect, the improvement of military leadership, particularly at the higher levels of the hierarchy, would have been more vital for the purpose of developing combat effectiveness for the RVNAF than any other program. At the higher levels, what the advisers sought most to do was establish good rapport with their counterparts rather than pressuring them to do the job. But, niceties and civility simply did not work when a war was being fought. As General James L. Collins, Jr. has so aptly commented on this problem:

> "The rapport approach is dangerous because it lends itself to the acceptance of substandard performance by the adviser. In any future situation where advisers are deployed under hostile conditions, the emphasis should be on getting the job done, not on merely getting along with the individual being advised."[1]

The US advisory effort suffered a setback during the first few years of active US participation in the war. The role of advisers was overshadowed by the presence of US combat forces on whom the success or failure of the war effort depended. ARVN units began to turn to US field commanders for operational guidance and support since it was they who wielded true military power, not the regular advisers who during this time acted mostly in a liaison role. Because of their reduced role and the priority of personnel assignment given to US combat forces, the selection of advisers was no longer subject to exacting criteria, and the advisory effectiveness suffered accordingly.

But it was also during this period that more consideration was given to pacification, and the advisory system was thus greatly expanded on a territorial basis. The availability of US advisers at the district level was truly beneficial for the pacification program and contributed substantially to the general war effort. The adviser at district level was a military officer but his encompassing duties required him to act in both military and civilian capacities. As a matter of fact he was a special kind of adviser. Because of the combat and social environment

---

[1] Brigadier General James Lawton Collins, Jr., *The Development and Training of the South Vietnamese Army, 1950 - 1972* (Department of the Army, Washington, D.C.: 1975) p. 130.

in which he lived and operated and the many and highly diversified problems he had to solve, the district adviser at the end of his tour had truly become a political-military adviser in his own right. The unique experience and invaluable training thus acquired by US officers might well make them more qualified leaders in future assignments.

The task of upgrading RF and PF combat effectiveness through the device of Mobile Assistance Teams was only reasonably successful. This was due less to the limitations of advisory personnel than to constraints of the territorial command and control system. Conceived and operating as part of the RVNAF, the RF and PF were nevertheless placed under a different command channel and more often than not were employed in a haphazard and unorthodox manner by a province or district chief who was always too busy with his administrative or political duties. Lacking strong and effective mainforce backing and adequate combat support, RF and PF were usually exposed to piecemeal defeat and seldom had the offensive spirit or the motivation required to accomplish their difficult mission.

On their part, the ARVN regular units did not fare much better, bound as they were to their territorial security and pacification support duties. Only rarely did they have the opportunity to evade the debilitating effect of routine activities and participate in mobile operations. Not until after 1968 was there any systematic effort to improve their combat effectiveness through intensive programs of combined operations. But by the time ARVN units really got off to a good start US forces were already standing down to redeploy.

In addition to the advisory effort, the presence of US combat forces in South Vietnam since 1965 also contributed substantially to upgrading the RVNAF and enabling the RVN government to consolidate its popular base and control. This contribution was made through combined operations jointly conducted by the RVNAF and US forces against enemy forces and bases. With a view to integrating all military efforts, emphasis was placed on cooperation and coordination between Vietnamese and American combat units. Short of a unified command, this was a good working solution to direct the common war effort although it was far from being ideal.

To provide guidance and direction for successful cooperation and coordination in operational matters, the RVNAF Joint General Staff and the US Military Assistance Command jointly worked out an annual Combined Campaign Plan which set forth the objectives, policies and procedures to be carried out by US Field Forces and ARVN Corps. The plan provided general guidelines for the common war effort but failed to institute any combined staff agency to monitor, supervise, and follow up on its actual conduct. These functions were performed separately by the JGS and MACV although cooperation and coordination were achieved through periodic combined command or staff meetings. It was apparently felt that such an arrangement was enough since the field commands were responsible for the actual planning and conduct of combat operations. Only in intelligence were there permanent combined agencies for analysis, production and dissemination.

During the early period from 1965 to 1968, various formulas were suggested but the actual combat cooperation and coordination effort at the field level was piecemeal and individualistic. It depended primarily on the personal rapport between counterpart commanders, the relative interest each of them took in the combined effort, and the tactical situation in each corps tactical zone. The role played by the RVNAF was, as a matter of fact, a passive one since they were made responsible only for territorial security and pacification support. It was the US forces that held the initiative in combat operations because they were assigned this mission and controlled all vital support assets. The division of tasks thus determined by the Combined Campaign plan reflected the status of the RVNAF during this period. Their combat effectiveness was marginal and their combat support assets were still very limited.

Aside from securing operations conducted by US forces around their bases, which necessarily involved elements of ARVN or territorial forces, large scale actions against enemy bases were almost exclusively planned and performed by US forces. In the few operations involving the participation of ARVN forces, Vietnamese units seldom numbered more than a few battalions which were either assigned objectives of secondary importance or served as blocking or cordon forces. The US Marines Combined Action in ICTZ was probably the first conscious effort at coordination and cooperation at the lowest echelon. Although its goal was to provide support for the pacification program and training for the Popular Forces, it certainly benefited US Marines forces by providing security for their bases. The first significant combined operational effort was Operation FAIRFAX whose success was due both to the long duration of the operation and the personal interest of the MACV commander himself.

In general, the combined effort during this period depended largely on the personality, policy and operational concept of each US Field Force Commander and, to a lesser extent, on the attitude of his ARVN counterpart. The degree of rapport between them was a factor that determined cooperation and coordination between their staffs and subordinate commands. If both American and Vietnamese field commanders were willing and shared a common enthusiasm for combined efforts, then cooperation and coordination automatically became a rule or practice between their staffs and units.

As has been said earlier, ARVN Corps commanders were usually deeply involved in administration and political matters and could not spare enough time or energy to devote to the tactical problems which, fortunately, were cared for by US Field Forces. The rare visits they made to subordinate units were always solemn, formal and time-consuming occasions that practically stopped all activities of the unit being visited. An ARVN Corps Commander never casually dropped in for a visit or for a working session with the unit commander. How could the Corps commander, in these circumstances, have a full grasp of the military situation in his own area of responsibility? Corps commanders were not interested in what US forces were doing, either. There were occasional visits to US forces, of course, but they were more in the nature of ceremonial or official functions. Although some claimed that US Field Forces withheld information concerning US plans and activities—which was probably true in a few instances—Corps commanders were never fully informed about the tactical situation and friendly activities, either Vietnamese or American. They depended totally on US initiative and efforts.

Corps staffs, as a consequence, were never required to make studies or plans to respond positively to the requirements of the situation. Most of the time Corps staffs performed tedious routine work on a day-to-day basis. Operational plans, therefore, were almost always initiated and worked out by US Field Force staffs. It was common knowledge that Corps operational plans during this period were more often than not merely translations or excerpts of US plans and orders.

On their part, US Field Force commanders were always devoted to and busy with their own duties and units. Despite their nominal capacity as Senior Corps Advisers, they rarely performed their advisory functions. The true adviser who worked closely with the Corps commander was always the Deputy Corps Adviser. The changeovers of US Field Force commanders also affected the adviser-counterpart relationship and by extension, the cooperation and coordination between ARVN and US forces. There were some exceptions; these were cases in which cooperation and coordination had been well established and where US commanders enjoyed a true prestige and trust with regard to their counterparts and Vietnamese troops.

At lower echelons, brigade or battalion, US unit commanders were generally reluctant to participate in combined operations with ARVN units. At these levels there existed no adviser-counterpart relationship between US and ARVN unit commanders. When they participated in combined operations, their relationship was usually one of mutual support—for the duration of the common effort. The reluctance to cooperate on the part of US brigade or battalion commanders derived chiefly from a prejudice against the combat effectiveness of ARVN units. They appeared not to realize that perseverance, determination and tolerance were the ingredients that were required from both sides to arrive at genuine cooperation.

Geographic location and terrain also affected cooperation. For a Corps which was responsible for a too large area such as the II CTZ, distance was really an impediment to the combined effort. Since II Corps and its divisions headquarters were located far from I Field Force and its subordinate units and because each of these units were assigned a separate area of responsibility, effective cooperation and coordination became a real problem. Some of the difficulties were overcome by good communications and by frequent combined command and staff meetings, but these were mainly useful for planning purposes. For a genuinely integrated effort to be effective on the basis of cooperation and coordination, there was also a requirement for constant supervision and follow-up by both commanders on the battlefield on a regular, if not daily basis. The best solution to achieve this would have been a fully integrated tactical operations center or at least the co-location of headquarters or command posts at every tactical level. The exchange of liaison teams between headquarters was a poor substitute for coordination by close physical proximity, because liaison teams obviously have their limits.

A major impediment for the RVNAF was the continuing lack of combat support assets and the perennial shortage of forces available for combined operations. Almost all assets required for the support of ARVN units were provided by US forces, from a command and liaison ship to airlift or helilift facilities, firepower, engineers, supplies, medical evacuation, etc. In large measure, therefore, combined operations depended on the availability of resources. This explained why they were usually initiated and planned by US forces. Then, in order to muster enough forces for the combined effort, it was usually necessary to redeploy ARVN units committed to pacification support. This was a step that neither the US Field Force commander nor the Corps commander took lightly, given the emphasis the RVN government placed on pacification and rural development at the time.

Not until after the successful counterattack by US and ARVN forces in the wake of the enemy 1968 Tet offensive did operational cooperation and coordination develop into a systematic and purposeful effort. This was basically due to a drastic change in American policy toward the war. The US was more and more inclined to curtail US participation and was turning over more combat responsibility to the RVNAF. Programs were initiated to quickly expand and modernize the RVNAF on the one hand and upgrade Vietnamese combat effectiveness on the other. This preparatory work was to pave the way for the Vietnamization program and the disengagement of US forces from South Vietnam.

The task of improving the RVNAF combat effectiveness became the major concern of MACV and US Field Forces. Since the trend of modern warfare emphasized airmobility and the effective use of firepower support, the US effort concentrated on training ARVN units in airmobile operations and the coordinated use of combat support assets. In contrast to the earlier period, combined operations involved an increasing number of ARVN units and were conducted more regularly within pre-conceived programs. At the same time, more modern weapons and equipment were made available to ARVN infantry divisions.

Following encouraging results achieved through the integrated employment of US and ARVN units by US XXIV Corps in the two northernmost provinces of I CTZ, I and II US Field Forces initiated extensive programs of combined operations in II and III Corps Tactical Zones. These programs, called "pair off" and "Dong Tien" respectively, have been discussed in Chapter V. In general, they substantially contributed to the rapid improvement of morale and combat effectiveness of ARVN units. For one thing, these programs offered Vietnamese unit commanders at all echelons a good opportunity to learn their trade. For another, they were a training method that no school or training center could duplicate in classrooms or even in field exercises. By working day and night side by side with US units, Vietnamese commanders were able to absorb several invaluable experiences in command and leadership that neither advisers nor schools could have provided. The advantages of these programs were evident. The only drawback was their short duration. One may wonder what these programs could have done to the RVNAF had they been initiated at the very beginning of the US participation in the war. Then perhaps, Vietnamization could have begun much earlier. And if, instead of a gradual response approach, the US had fully and resolutely brought its entire military might to bear on the war effort, then surely the outcome of the war would have been different.

The advent of combined operations also helped to some extent to mitigate the problem of shortage of capable cadre at all echelons. Those ARVN units which were most exposed to US tutelage and had several opportunities to operate alongside US units, such as the 1st and 22d

Infantry Divisions, for example, were all able to develop a very cohesive and uniformly capable command cadre. In addition, they also acquired good traditions and a solid reputation as proven combat units. The high degree of success in these instances, however, depended more on the genuine interest and close association that US commanders displayed toward ARVN units than anything else. An outstanding example was found in the tactical area of responsibility of the US XXIV Corps where cooperation and coordination were neither formally instituted under any formalized program nor bound by any procedure or rule. The key to success here was the US commander himself who daily visited and made himself available to ARVN units on a permanent basis. It was his personal care for the needs and well-being of ARVN troops that made them feel as familiar and as close to him as to their own commander.

On the other hand, when ARVN units directly cooperated with US forces on a permanent basis, their higher commands usually became complacent and less active. All that they had to do was monitor, follow up, and be satisfied with results and reports. The task of planning and conducting operations was entrusted to divisions and regiments and to whatever arrangements for coordination and cooperation they made with US units. This passivity in leadership and planning in time turned into a major deficiency which became more acute when US forces began to redeploy and which adversely affected both morale and combat effectiveness of the RVNAF.

Trained and accustomed as they were to US resources and standards, ARVN units naturally acquired skills and proficiency in the employment of modern combat support assets. This posed no problem as long as US forces were there, since they supplied what the RVNAF were unable to provide. What was questionable in the long run was the own ability of the RVNAF to provide support assets at the same level and rate once US forces were withdrawn. The most serious drawback seemed to be an ingrained habit of overkilling by profligate use of firepower and the over-dependence of ARVN unit commanders on tactical air support, particularly B-52 strikes.

In retrospect, as has been said earlier, the combined operations effort initiated by US forces to upgrade the RVNAF combat effectiveness and as preparation to turn over the combat responsibility to the RVNAF should have been encouraged much earlier, when US Field Forces were activated. Since the combined effort was in essence a joint enterprise at all levels, the question was why had it not been attempted also at higher levels. To have good combat troops and adequate support resources was certainly not enough. There should also have been stronger leadership, more effective planning, better command and control, and more profound motivation. ARVN Corps staffs and even the JGS could have been given the opportunity to learn, too. Why limit the training to lower levels? It did not make sense to have old fashioned and lackadaisical commanders in charge of advanced and modern troops.

In general, despite shortcomings and drawbacks, the US presence and effort truly helped the RVNAF to improve in most aspects. In return, US commanders, and advisers in particular, learned something about the complex nature of the Vietnam war and acquired invaluable experience that might be helpful to them in some future conflict. There remains though a fundamental question regarding the Vietnam conflict. Why was there a failure to produce strong leadership and motivation? This was, in the final analysis, what plagued the RVNAF the most. To be able to answer this question requires a thorough knowledge of the nature of the war, the kind of political system that directed the war effort, and the circumstances that affected leadership and motivation. A full answer to why there was such a profound lack of strong leadership and adequate motivation lies in these characteristics of the war, its politics, and its circumstances. It can be said though that good leadership and motivation were definitely not developed to an adequate extent and that this failure had a disastrous effect on the eventual outcome of the war.

Glossary

ABN	Airborne
ACD	Air Cavalry Division (US)
A & DSLC	Administrative and Direct Support Logistics Company (at least one per province for support of RF-PF)
AK-47	Soviet 7.62-mm assault rifle
ALC	Area Logistical Command
AO	Area of Operation
APC	Armored Personnel Carrier
ARVN	Army of the Republic of Vietnam. Common abbreviation used to refer to regular Army forces to include airborne and ranger units.
AT	Antitank
Buddy Operations	Combined operations by US and South Vietnamese forces.
CAC	Combined Action Company
CAG	Combined Action Group
CAP	Combined Action Platoon
CAT	Combat Assistance Team
CAV	Cavalry (US)
CDEC	Combined Document Exploitation Center
CICV	Combined Intelligence Center, Vietnam
CLC	Central Logistic Command
CMAC	Capital Military Assistance Command
CMD or CMR	Capital Military District or Region
CMEC	Combined Materiel Exploitation Center
CMIC	Combined Military Interrogation Center

COMUSMACV	Commander, United States Military Assistance Command, Vietnam
Cordon and Search	Operation to seal off and search an area
CORDS	Civil Operations and Revolutionary Development Support. A MACV organization that provided single manager direction of all US civil/military RD activities in the Republic of Vietnam.
COSVN	Central Office of South Vietnam
CP	Command Post
CSCC	Combat Support Coordination Center
CT	Abbreviation of Cong Truong, term used by the VC to designate divisions activated under COSVN
CTC	Central Training Command
CTZ	Corps Tactical Zone. The geographical area of responsibility of a Corps, but frequently used to refer to the Corps Headquarters itself.
CUPP	Combined Unit Pacification Program
DMAC	Delta Military Assistance Command (MR4)
DMZ	Demilitarized Zone
DS	Direct Support
DSA	District Senior Advisor
DTA	Division Tactical Area. The geographical area of responsibility of a division, frequently used to refer to the Division Headquarters itself.
FDC	Fire Direction Center
FFV or FFORCEV	Field Forces, Vietnam (US)
FO	Forward Observer (Artillery)
FSB	Fire Support Base
FSE	Forward Support Element
FWMAF	Free World Military Assistance Forces
GS	General Support
GPWD	General Political Warfare Department
GVN	Government of South Vietnam
J-2	Assistant Chief of Staff, Intelligence

JGS	Joint General Staff (RVNAF)
JOC	Joint Operations Center
JUSPAO	Joint United States Public Affairs Office. Served US interests as well as advising the GVN in information and psychological operations.
KIA	Killed in Action
LNO	Liaison Officer
LOC	Lines Of Communication
Local force	Viet Cong combat unit subordinate to a district or province
LRRP	Long Range Reconnaissance Patrol
LTL	Vietnamese Interprovincial Route (Lien Tinh Lo)
LZ	Landing Zone
M-16	US light weight, rapid-firing 5.56-mm rifle
MACV	Military Assistance Command, Vietnam
MAF	Marine Amphibious Force (US)
Main force	Viet Cong and North Vietnamese military units subordinate to the Central Office of South Vietnam, military regions, or other higher echelons of command.
MAT	Mobile Advisory Team
MEDCAP	Medical Civic Action Program
MEDEVAC	Medical Evacuation
MI	Military Intelligence
MILPHAP	Military Provincial Health Assistance Program
MP	Military Police
MR	Military Region
MSS	Military Security Service (Vietnamese)
MTT	Mobile Training Team
NATO	North Atlantic Treaty Organization
NPFF	National Police Field Force
NT	Abbreviation of Nong Truong, alternate term used by the VC to designate a division.

NVA	North Vietnamese Army
Pattern Activity Analysis	Procedure begun in mid-1966 which consists of detailed plotting on maps of information on enemy activity obtained from a variety of sources over an extended period of time.
PF	Popular Force (s). Military forces locally recruited, employed within their home district and organized into platoons.
PICC	Province Intelligence Coordination Committee
PRU	Provincial Reconnaissance Unit
PSA	Province Senior Adviser
PSDF	People's Self Defense Forces
PsyOps	Psychological Warfare Operations
PW	Prisoner of War
QL	Vietnamese National Route (Quoc Lo)
RD	Rural or Revolutionary Development
RF	Regional Force (s). Military forces recruited and employed within a Province.
ROK	Republic of Korea
RPG-2	Soviet antitank grenade launcher designated B-40 by the VC.
RR	Recoilless Rifle
RVN	Republic of Vietnam. Sometimes used interchangeable with GVN when referring to the government or with SVN when referring to the country.
RVNAF	Republic of Vietnam Armed Forces
SAPOV	Sub-Area Petroleum Office, Vietnam
Search-and-clear	Offensive military operation designed to sweep through an area with the objective of locating, driving out, or destroying the enemy.
Search-and-destroy	Offensive operation designed to seek out and destroy enemy forces, headquarters, and supply installation, with emphasis on destruction rather than occupation.
SLAR	Side Looking Airborne Radar
SVN	South Vietnam. Generally connotes the land itself.

TAOI	Tactical Area of Interest
TAOR	Tactical Area of Responsibility
TL	Vietnamese Provincial Route (Tinh Lo)
TOC	Tactical Operations Center
USAID	United States Agency for International Development
USARV	United States Army, Vietnam
USOM	United States Operations Mission, a precursor of USAID
USMACV	United States Military Assistance Command, Vietnam.
VC	Viet Cong. Communist insurgents in South Vietnam
VCI	Viet Cong Infrastructure
VHF	Very High Frequency
VNAF	Vietnam Air Force
VNN	Vietnam Navy

www.ingramcontent.com/pod-product-compliance
Lightning Source LLC
Chambersburg PA
CBHW080543170426
43195CB00016B/2660